Trench Art:
A Brief History and Guide, 1914-1939

TRENCH ART:
A BRIEF HISTORY & GUIDE,
1914-1939

Nicholas J Saunders

LEO COOPER

In Memory of

WILLIAM, MATTHEW, JAMES & JACK,
all of whom fought and survived

First published in Great Britain in 2001 by Leo Cooper
an imprint of Pen & Sword Books Limited
47 Church Street, Barnsley, South Yorkshire S70 2AS

Copyright © Nicholas J Saunders, 2001

*For up-to date information on other titles produced under the Pen & Sword imprint,
please telephone or write to:*
Pen & Sword Books Limited
FREEPOST
47 Church Street
Barnsley
South Yorkshire
S70 2BR

Telephone (24 hours): 01226 734555

ISBN 0-85052-793-7 Cased Edition

ISBN 0-85052-820-8 Paperback Edition

British Library Cataloguing in Publication Data

Printed by CPI UK

Contents

Acknowledgements

In a book such as this there are, inevitably, many people from all walks of life who have generously given their help and advice, criticism, encouragement, company, and rare insight. A full list of how each person has aided my research would be a chapter in itself, and so I would like to offer my heartfelt thanks equally to all of the following who, each in their own way, made this book possible.

Paul Cornish (Imperial War Museum), Peter Liddle (Liddle Collection, The Second World War Experience Centre), Jenny Spencer-Smith and Oliver Buckley (National Army Museum), and the curators of innumerable Regimental Museums throughout the United Kingdom who kindly responded to my letters, questionnaires and requests for photographs. Marion Wenzel (Bosnia-Hercegovina Heritage Rescue, London and Sarajevo), Peter Doyle (University of Greenwich), Jay Winter and John Carman (Cambridge University), Jeremy Coote and Marius Kwint (Oxford University), Mark Dennis (Museum of the United Grand Lodge, London), John Schofield (English Heritage), Danny Miller, Suzanne Küchler, Hugh Clout, Mike Rowlands, Christopher Tilley, and Barbara Bender, all at University College London, Annette Becker (Paris X Nanterre), Thomas Compère-Morel and Marie-Pascale Prévost-Bault (L'Historial de la Grande Guerre, Péronne), Peter Aitken and Jane Peek (Australian War Memorial, Canberra), Mark Derez (Katholick University, Leuven), Franky Bostyn and Johan Vandewalle (Association for Battlefield Archaeology in Flanders, Zonnebeke), Aleks Deseyne (Atlantic Walls, Raversijde, Ostend), Jan Dewilde (Stedelijke Museum, Ieper), Chatham Dockyard Historical Society, Marie-Monique Huss (University of Westminster, London), and Peter Taylor.

Also, Gil Goutsmit (Ostend), Roger Lampaert (Zillebeke), Gabriel Versavel (Passendale), Senior Captain A. Vander Mast (Langemark-Poelkapelle), Lieutenant Colonel L. Deprez-Wouts (Ieper), John Woolsgrove and Christine De Deyne (The Shell Hole, Ieper), Alain and Wilma Bouten (The Protea, Geluvelt-Zonnebeke), Philipe Oosterlinck, Joe Lagae, Roger De Smul (Hooge), Jacques Schier (Hill 62), Rik Ryon (Proven), Ivan Sinnaeve (Sint-Jan), Laurie Farrow (Messines), Peter Barton, Ken Dunn, James Brazier, Bill Abbitt, Steve Rarity, Ralph Thompson, Angela Kelsall, Bernard Hepton, Christopher Basey, T.M.D. Ball, Jane Kimball, Roy Butler, Paul Hamilton, Stefany Tomalin,

Gordon Rae, Pamela Caunt, Jon Price, Bill Chandler, Phil Reeve, Gerry O'Connell, the late Joe Lyndhurst and various others who, at their own request, remain anonymous.

I am especially grateful to University College London for the opportunity to undertake the research upon which this book is based, and above all to The British Academy, for the award of an Institutional Fellowship, which made it possible. I owe a great debt to my wife Pauline and my children Roxanne and Alexander who suffered (or enjoyed) my frequent absences, and the gradual filling up of their home with strange objects. To my parents I am grateful for the various pieces of Trench Art they have acquired for me over recent years.

Obtaining photographs for this book has been its own adventure. Except where stated, all are my copyright (c). Where copyright is mine but permissions were granted by others, this is so noted. I am particularly grateful to Gabriel Versavel for permission to photograph his family collection and to reproduce some of these here, where they are jointly credited to the Versavel Archive.

Finally, I am proud to thank my grandfathers, Alfred William Saunders of the King's Own Royal Regiment (Lancaster), and Matthew Inkerman Chorley of the South Lancashire Regiment and his brothers James and Jack Chorley, all of whom fought in the Great War and survived, though not without scars. To them, and all the makers of Great War Trench Art I dedicate this book. *Ars longa, vita brevis* indeed!

About this book

This book is called a brief history and guide – a guide, that is, to historical meanings and significances rather than commercial values. In one sense it has been a long time coming as, to my knowledge, it is the first book ever published in English on Trench Art. As with many books on the Great War, there is a personal element – one which involves half-remembered stories of grandfathers and uncles, and visceral images of the war from my own childhood.

My first memories of the Great War of 1914-1918 were of settling down on a Friday night with my maternal grandfather to watch the BBC's monumental series *The Great War* during the 1960s. Week after week I watched, fascinated, as boys of my generation often were, at the flickering black and white images of the war – the incredible bombardments, soldiers clambering over the top and young faces grown old before their time, staring blankly into the camera's eye. Yet, not once during this time do I recall my grandfather making any comment which might have indicated

that he had been part of these scenes of carnage and destruction. In fact, like so many of his generation, he never spoke of it at all. He preferred to remember his days travelling the world as a Merchant Seaman after the war. Throughout my childhood my view of him was framed by a photograph on his living room shelf – a dapper young man dressed in white, standing nonchalantly on the deck of HMS *Homeric*.

Only later, years after his death, did I discover that the splendidly named Matthew Inkerman Chorley had been a private in the 1/5th Battalion of the South Lancashire Regiment. He had fought at the start of the Third Battle of Ypres (Passchendaele) in July 1917, and had escaped death by a whisker when the rest of his battalion had been wiped

Fig. 1: Private Matthew Inkerman Chorley (seated).

out in a German counter-attack at the Banteux Ravine north of Épéhy in September of the same year. He had been paid extra as a 'First Class Shot' and had spent many months after the war working in a military hospital at Wimereux near Boulogne. These things were unknown to me when he was alive and, like many others who discover similar facts about their family, the serendipitous nature of one's own existence becomes a strange food for thought.

During the many hours spent watching The Great War, a shiny metal object had sat on the mantelpiece, lit by the flickering coal fire beneath. At sometime I must have noticed it – the flat brass surface decorated with two halves of a bullet flanking a metal button, and a simple inscription – 'France 1919'. Previously it had been on the mantelpiece in my great-grandmother's house where my mother had remembered seeing it always brightly polished. After my great-grandmother died, it had passed to Matthew and once again took up its position, this time on his mantelpiece.

Fig. 2: Brass matchbox cover that stood on my grandfather's mantelpiece throughout my childhood.

Somewhere along the way I learned that it was a matchbox cover of a kind commonly made by soldiers during their wartime service. When he died in 1984 the matchbox continued its journey, passing to me, and went straight into a drawer.

In 1996, while researching my family history, and particularly the wartime service of my grandfathers, I remembered the matchbox cover and placed it, duly polished, on the mantelpiece next to a recently discovered photograph of him in uniform. One day, I looked at it not as a grandson but as an anthropologist, and was intrigued. I felt sure that somewhere there was an expert, perhaps several, who had spent a lifetime studying this kind of object – after all, the libraries were full of books on every aspect of the First World War. Somewhere there must be articles, books and photographs which described and analysed these objects which seemed to me now to resonate strongly with the war and its aftermath for soldiers and their loved ones.

Phone calls and letters to museums, universities and well-known authors on the war in the United Kingdom and beyond proved fruitless and intriguing at the same time. The answers to my questions were always the same – the material is called 'Trench Art', though it wasn't made in the trenches; there are no experts, there is no research of any kind, no articles, no contemporary photographs and no books. Many museums had items which could be described as Trench Art, but only a few had any on display, and these were as examples of what soldiers did in their spare time. It quickly became apparent that in eighty odd years no one had given these objects any serious thought. The general feeling was that nothing could be done with this heterogeneous mass of things – they were simply anonymous objects which it was impossible to categorize or make any sense of. They were the oddities of war.

It occurred to me that this could not be so. These objects, like any others made by people throughout history, had stories to tell, though at the time I had no idea how astonishing some of these would be. The research upon which this book draws, proved to be more than just an investigation of strange and curious things – it was an exploration of objects and people, and the memories and meanings which link them. In a way, it is a kind of archaeology – excavating the lives of my own family, as well as those of a generation whose menfolk fought, died and suffered, in 'The Great War for Civilization'.

Introduction

The First World War was a turning point in human history. It shattered an old world of confident traditions and attitudes, and ushered in a new era of industrialized war that has come to define our modern world. Between 1914 and 1918 the 'Great War for Civilization', as the conflict was ironically called, gave birth to ways of life which those who lived through its momentous years could not possibly have foreseen. In many ways, it destroyed the kind of European civilization which it was fought to maintain.

Today, as the old millenium slips into history and a new century begins, the Great War and its legacy is being reassessed, not only by those who study military and cultural history, but also by archaeologists and anthropologists. The new, wider perspectives brought by these disciplines seek answers to different kinds of questions, particularly concerning the ordinary soldiers' and civilians' experiences of war, and the psychological, political, economic, geographical and technological legacies of the conflict. It is these new approaches which, by exploring deeper, perhaps universal issues, are beginning to add to our understanding of the cultural memory of twentieth century war.

One aspect of this renewed and reoriented interest focuses on the relationship between people and the things they make – objects which capture a spark of the human spirit in the extreme conditions of total war. This is a timely development, as the First World War set a precedent for all subsequent conflicts by virtue of being above all, a war of technology, of matériel.

So much has been written about the Great War that it is difficult to believe there exists a topic which has not been exhaustively investigated, or even acknowledged. Yet this has been the fate of 'Trench Art' – a term applied to a huge variety of objects of metal, wood, cloth, bone and stone, made by soldiers and civilians alike between 1914 and 1939. Items made from such materials include decorated artillery shellcases, bullet-crucifixes, letter-openers, cigarette lighters and pens made from shrapnel and cartridges, and artful miniature aeroplanes and tanks, as well as talismanic jewellery – rings, bracelets and brooches. Other examples, such as elaborate embroideries, beadwork and carved wood, were also made, sometimes to raise money, or as therapeutic handiwork by soldiers recovering from shell shock, or coming to terms with disability.

It is surprising that in the vast literature on the Great War there is hardly a mention of these objects which were known to every soldier and their families during the war and inter-war years. This oversight has been due partly to the inability (combined with disinterest) of traditional approaches to the war to take these objects seriously. Hitherto, these approaches have emphasized military tactics, victories and blunders, and the often tragic circumstances and consequences of battles on the Somme, at Passchendaele or Gallipoli. Such accounts have concentrated on the big picture, and have argued endlessly over the rights and wrongs of particular military actions, and the conduct of the war. At the other extreme, personal recollections of these events by the soldiers themselves have added a new and textured dimension to our understanding of the war. Yet even the remarkable accounts by Lyn Macdonald and others have only rarely mentioned the objects which mediated the human experience of war.

Consequently, Trench Art has been 'invisible in plain view' for over eighty years – slipping through the net of the many books, articles, exhibitions and television programmes on the war. Yet, in a very real sense, these objects and the battlefield landscapes in which they were produced, are the raw materials of future archaeologies. They are part of our cultural heritage – an indispensable element in the search for understanding of how soldiers and civilians comprehend and come to terms with the intensities which modern war imposes on them. Such objects provide glimpses into what can be called the missing history of the Great War and, by extension to other conflicts, into the nature of war itself. For, as all soldiers know, battlefield killing is only one part (albeit the most intense) of the many experiences which make up a soldier's wartime life.

At the moment, the variety of objects known as Trench Art are not rare, though they are becoming ever more difficult to find. For the most part, and with some notable exceptions, they are not sealed beneath glass display cabinets nor buried deep in dingy museum storerooms. They are in fact, ever present in the world around us. In many houses in Britain, Belgium, France and beyond, they still stand on mantelpieces, bookshelves and in hallways or, more often perhaps, are boxed away in garages and lofts. In this respect, they are unique artefacts – recognized and owned by millions of people who know nothing of the Great War but who vaguely recall some strange object bequeathed by a grandfather or uncle, and tucked away somewhere in the labyrinth of the home.

Beyond the domestic setting, Trench Art lives on as a miscellaneous group of objects in the thriving trade in military collectables. Here they are bought and sold on a daily basis by dealers, collectors and the curious across Europe, the United States, Canada, Australia, New Zealand and elsewhere, in militaria fairs, flea markets, car-boot sales, antique shops and auction rooms, as well as in cyberspace over the Internet.

Trench Art is one of those rare events in history – a mass of objects which played a variety of sometimes ordinary, sometimes extraordinary, roles for people living in extraordinary times, yet which by their humble nature have been overlooked, ignored or dismissed in innumerable accounts of the events which gave them birth. In other words, Trench Art is a uniquely informative but so far undocumented resource.

In this book, my aim is to reclaim a little of Trench Art's significance, to document its types and explore its previously unrecognized social and perhaps even spiritual and symbolic dimensions. The first aim is one which many people, especially dealers and collectors, have thought long overdue. The second may come as a surprise. Yet it is this interpretive aspect which makes possible and enriches the description which precedes it. In the past, purely descriptive accounts of Trench Art have been defeated by the sheer numbers and types of objects. Partly for this reason, and to my knowledge, no book in English has ever been published on the topic. My approach, as an anthropologist rather than a military historian or collector, is concerned with the significance and contexts of the objects as well as their different kinds, and highlights the meanings of diversity in the techniques employed to make them, and of the conditions under which they were made. It is an almost forensic approach which allows for a classification of Trench Art's variety of forms and of their associations to be made.

Origins and perspectives

As an idea, Trench Art did not begin with the First World War, though its name is forever associated with the trenches which have become that conflict's most recognizable feature. For as long as humans have fought wars they have recycled and reused the objects and materials of war for peaceful ends – the 'swords into ploughshares' philosophy. Such objects seem to be a universal human response to the varied experiences of war, from Roman soldiers idling their time away on Hadrian's Wall to the magnificent objects of bone and straw made by Napoleonic prisoners of war incarcerated across England during the early nineteenth century. War is a characteristic of all civilizations, and the habit of re-working its raw materials seems to have been a similarly universal phenomenon.

The immediate predecessors of Great War Trench Art can be found throughout the nineteenth century, beginning with the Napoleonic wars (1796-1815), followed by the Crimean (1854-5), American Civil (1861-5), Franco-Prussian (1870-1), Spanish-American (1898) and Boer wars (1899-1902). All of these produced Trench Art of a kind – from the human faces and pornographic scenes carved into the soft lead of .69 calibre rifle balls by both sides in the American Civil War, to fluted and punch-decorated artillery shell cases of the Spanish-American conflict, and the wooden matchholder inscribed with 'From the Teak of HMS *Terrible* whose guns relieved Ladysmith' from the

Fig. 3: Hotel reception bell in the shape of a German pickelhaube helmet from the Franco-Prussian War.

Boer War. Many other kinds of similar objects were made in innumerable smaller and less well documented conflicts associated with this era of continental strife, exploration and imperialism. However, even this more recent historical aspect of Trench Art must lay beyond the scope of this book.

It was the experience of something new and terrible in human history which produced the greatest flowering of Trench Art. Industrialized war on a global scale was perhaps an unforseen consequence of the Industrial Revolution. Unforeseen that is in the sense that, as the First World War so tragically proved, new technologies had run ahead of traditional military thinking. While generals and politicians struggled to come to terms with a kind of war with which they were totally unfamiliar, and for which they were quite unprepared, the fighting man was subjected to horrors which he could not begin to comprehend. The place of the Great War in our collective historical consciousness is unique by virtue of the paradoxes and ironies which attended the tragic and hitherto undreamt of scale of death and maiming. For the first time in history, this included hundreds of thousands of men who simply vanished from the face of the earth – vapourized and blown to pieces by high explosive – and commemorated now on monuments to 'The Missing', and symbolized by the 'Unknown Soldier'.

It is against this background that every object which can be described as Trench Art tells a story of the momentous experiences of its maker – whether a front line soldier, prisoner of war or civilian refugee. In the Great War, these objects resonate with the terrors of endless bombardment, night raids, gas attacks, boredom and the bestial nature of trench life. While these experiences are described in vivid language in the works of Edmund Blunden, Siegfried Sassoon, Wilfred Owen, Robert Graves and others, the Trench Art objects which embodied them have remained silent and, for the main part, invisible.

Quite separate from soldiers' experiences, are the equally poignant associations of countless bereaved relatives, wives, lovers and friends, who went on pilgrimages to the battlefield cemeteries and memorials between 1919 and 1939 and who purchased Trench Art and other items as heart-rending souvenirs in acts of remembrance of their loved ones. Many such items were taken home and kept as household ornaments for the rest of their lives as ever present reminders of husbands, sons, fathers and sweethearts, who never returned.

This simple fact elevates Trench Art to something more than miscellaneous doodlings of soldiers. It envelops them in the flow of history, surrounds them with personal memories and suggests they have an untold story to tell. It casts doubt on the accuracy of the name Trench Art, and reveals that these objects were of many different kinds, made and used by different people, for a variety of reasons – for sale, barter and personal use. There were also unacknowledged deeper meanings, associated with spirituality, grief and mourning, relief and sometimes guilt at surviving when so many did not. It comes as a surprise to many people to learn that the majority of metal Trench Art items were made during the inter-war years (1919-1939) rather than during the war itself. It is perhaps even more surprising to learn that this is an ongoing tradition in areas affected by the Great War. From Belgium to Bosnia, decorated shells, pens, cigarette lighters and other items are still being made from the recycled metals of war.

Knowing this, it is probably less surprising to discover that Trench Art, in the purposefully wide definition adopted below, was also a feature of virtually every other twentieth century conflict. The Second World War, though a war of movement rather than trenches, had its own varieties, many of which were made by prisoners of war and those condemned to Nazi concentration camps. After 1945, many distinctive objects were made during conflicts in Korea, Vietnam and Bosnia – as well as in many smaller but equally bitter and problematical conflicts, such as the wooden weapons and embroidered and painted handkerchiefs made by members of the IRA inside Long Kesh in Northern Ireland, and objects fashioned from land mines in Afghanistan. Trench Art is revealed as a universal human response to the pressures and consequences of armed conflict, however designated. It is also, and fundamentally, a way in which the individual can express himself in three dimensions – objects in miniature of his experiences of life in armed struggle.

Trench Art has many stories to tell, though only those which relate to the Great War can be told here. It is clear that these objects, which for so long have been literally and metaphorically consigned to the furthest boundaries of the war, if not the rubbish bin, are in fact a hitherto untapped resource for exploring the human aspects of the Great War and its aftermath. At a time when Britain's annual Remembrance Day ceremony and its associated two minutes silence seems to be gathering more public support, it is perhaps time to acknowledge the lessons of Trench Art. These definitive objects of the Great War should be valued as a testament to the skills and fortitude of human beings under the almost unbearable pressures of modern war. Each item, however humble, is a potential symbol of the human spirit in extrem-is.

In many ways, the modern world was forged in the crucibles of war. Our

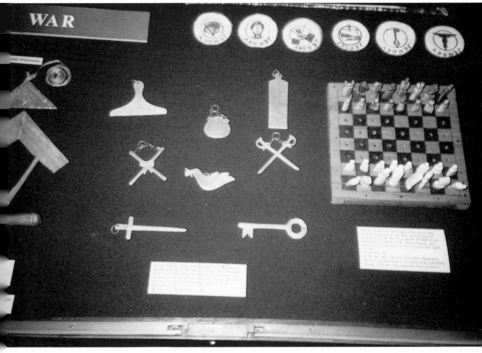

Fig. 4: Trench Art Chess set made from toothbrush handles and teak; Masonic jewels made by Freemason PoWs during the Second World War.

Fig. 5: Huey helicopter gunship made recently from Vietnamese Coca Cola can in imitation of Trench Art originals from the Vietnam War.

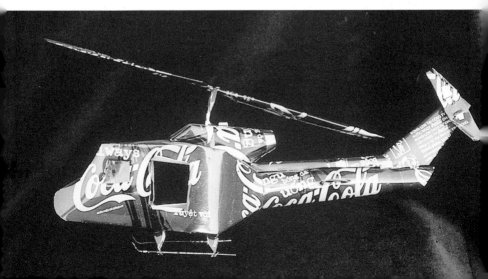

technological sophistication and the ease of life which we enjoy today did not come free. It was paid for in millions of lives and unimaginable suffering during the twentieth century's many conflicts, but particularly the First and Second World Wars. In some ways, perhaps, by reclaiming Trench Art's rightful place in the history of the Great War and inter-war years, a voice is restored to all those who suffered and died, and a small part of the debt that the living owe the dead is discharged.

Fig. 6: Trench Art is a living tradition in the Balkans.

Chapter 1

WHAT IS TRENCH ART?

'Trench Art' is the evocative but misleading name applied to the dazzling array of objects made by soldiers, prisoners of war and civilians from the waste of industrialized war, and a host of miscellaneous materials. Although, as already mentioned, such objects have probably been made throughout history, today the name mainly refers to items of the First World War. Even here, however, there are as many definitions of Trench Art as there are collectors, dealers and museum curators. The sheer number and variety of objects which can be considered, means that previous attempts to define what is and what is not Trench Art have been vague and contentious. This problem has been compounded by the fact that, while the term originates with the archetypal feature of First World War battlefields, it has been, and continues to be, applied to a host of similar objects from many different wars in which, for the most part, trenches played little or no part.

The thorny issue of definition lies at the heart of any serious consideration of Trench Art and has led to many different names being applied to the genre. The choices are legion and confusing. In Britain, the Imperial War Museum allocates Trench Art objects to its Department of Exhibits and Firearms, the National Army Museum refers to the material as 'Decorative Arts', the Royal Airforce Museum labels it 'Commemorative Art' and the National Maritime Museum keeps its examples in its Antiquities Department. The Museum of the United Grand Lodge of England regards its Trench Art in the same way as other items in its collections, and refers to them all as 'Masonic Jewels'. All of these names have their own history and appropriateness, and each reflects a conscious decision on the part of the museum concerned to classify objects which do not fit easily into any particular category.

Throughout the United Kingdom, there are over a hundred small regimental museums, all of whose curators recognize the term Trench Art but rightly question its validity and definition. Further muddying the waters is the fact that Trench Art is sometimes referred to as 'Soldier Art', and on occasion may be sub-divided into loose categories described as kinds of 'Folk Art', 'Refugee Art' or 'Prisoner of War Art'.

Some items remain 'invisible' as miscellaneous objects associated with innumerable pre-twentieth century conflicts.

The author has decided to keep the name Trench Art as a convenient term, mainly because of its widespread use and the instant (if disputed) recognition by many people of the kind of material it represents. In my view, what is important is to define the term as precisely as possible so that it can be used as accurately as possible, rather than invent another name or breathe life into one of the lesser known terms. Equally important, is to recognize that Trench Art is more than a name, it is a concept. Identifying it as such has far reaching consequences for how these objects are regarded and valued. After some eighty-five years, clarifying these issues must be a primary objective of this book.

The problem of trying to agree a definition of Trench Art is related in no small part to the astonishing diversity of the materials which qualify in one sense or another. Being as old as war itself, the idea of Trench Art brings a vast number of objects into view. Any attempt to make sense of this mass of artefacts, and to refine the hitherto catch-all nature of the term Trench Art, requires a working definition. In order to be as inclusive as possible yet also to keep some control over the material the following definition has been adopted – though hopefully this will be refined in the future. In this book, Trench Art is considered as <u>any object made by soldiers, prisoners of war and civilians, from war matériel or any other material, as long as object and maker are associated in time and space with armed conflict or its consequences.</u>

With this definition in mind, Trench Art associated with the First World War includes objects made at any time from 1914 to 1939, for reasons which will become clear later. It embraces the obvious instances of objects made from recycled war matériel such as artillery shell cases, detonators, bullets, grenades, shrapnel, ship and aircraft parts, as well as a host of unidentified scrap. It also includes commercially made metal items which have been personalized artistically, such as painted helmets, cigarette cases and lighters, weapons and writing materials. Apart from metal, also included are objects made from beads, embroidered and painted cloth, and innumerable items of carved wood, bone and stone. Each kind of object, the style of its decoration, and the more or less sophisticated techniques employed to make it, have a story to tell.

By adopting such an approach, it can be seen that while the boundaries of Trench Art are, by the nature of the material, somewhat fluid, important distinctions can be made. As an illustrative example, let us consider two kinds of object made specifically for killing or wounding – an edged weapon (sword, dagger or bayonet) and an artillery shell.

The edged weapon may have been decoratively engraved as part of the commercial manufacturing process. In my definition, this would not be Trench Art, as it would not be tied to a specific (or indeed any) conflict situation. However, if the blade had been individually decorated, i.e. personalized, in the time frame of a battle or war, this could qualify as Trench Art. Similarly, if fragments of such a weapon were integrated into some new shape or form – by anyone and anywhere – and during that same time frame, this would also qualify. The difference is important because of the associations and meanings attached to the item. There would be no meaningful associations or stories if the decoration was simply part of an anonymous commercial manufacturing process. But what stories there might be if the decoration was made by a soldier in a dugout, a refugee trying to make ends meet or a prisoner of war desperate to earn a little extra money.

The same approach can be adopted for the definitive weapon of the Great War – the artillery shell. To my knowledge, these weapons were never engraved by the men and women who manufactured them in the munitions factory (though missives to the Tommies at the front were sometimes slipped into a box of shells). Yet, if they had been, this would not be considered Trench Art. Once the live shells were being loaded into their artillery pieces ready for firing, soldiers often chalked on a caricature of the Kaiser or Hindenburg, or spelt out a message to the enemy – whether this be 'Here's one for you Fritz', or 'Remember the Lusitania'. In a very basic way this represented a kind of Trench Art – an artistic elaboration, perhaps ironic transformation – of a deadly weapon. After the shell had been fired and the empty shell case picked up and more permanently shaped or decorated this would obviously be Trench Art. With both these examples, it is not only the decoration which makes something into Trench Art, but also who did it and in what circumstances. This seems to me a fundamental point which differentiates personalized and meaningful creation from anonymous industrial production.

Considered in this way, Trench Art is revealed as a rich and untapped resource which can be investigated and considered from an anthropological perspective as well as from the more usual approaches of military history, social history and art history. For more than eighty years, traditional approaches to the Great War have ignored or denigrated Trench Art. The wider more inclusive approach of anthropology allows for the consideration of the most important issue – the relationship between the people and objects of the Great War. By looking at the context or circumstances of the making of an object, and for the main part ignoring the misleading innacuracy of the term Trench Art, we can see that objects made between 1919 and 1939 are as much a part (in the sense of being a legacy) of the Great War as those items made between 1914 and 1918.

Such an approach appears a fundamentally worthwhile endeavour – far more so than a straightforward collector's guide to a miscellaneous mass of unusual but mute objects. It might be argued that a consideration of the issues which lay behind this book open the door to a greater study – one which focuses on the relationship of all human beings to the materiality of war throughout human history.

The meanings of Trench Art

Having made a case for my approach to Trench Art, it can be seen that these objects are rich in symbolism and irony, their variety bearing more than silent witness to war. Individually and collectively, they possess a value beyond their common status as ephemera, curios and collectables. Equally obvious is the fact that the way such objects have been regarded hitherto has not only made the collector's life difficult, but has denied the true status of Trench Art as a body of meaningful objects capable of yielding unique insights into the nature of war.

The variety of meanings which different kinds of Trench Art possess have already been alluded to. Some are obvious, others less so. Where some aspects of an object's significance illustrate the ways in which anthropology can contribute to our understanding of the Great War, other aspects show how important such objects can be for the disciplines of anthropology and, in associated ways, for archaeology. As mentioned earlier, both these disciplines are becoming ever more concerned with the physical remains and cultural aspects of twentieth century war.

Chapter five explores the wider, and in many ways unfamiliar, aspects of what can be called the 'social worlds' of Trench Art. It it appropriate, however, to outline these ideas here so that in chapter two, which offers a classification of these objects, the reader is already familiar with some of the ideas and possible associations which Trench Art possesses.

Trench Art objects embody experiences of war which are not always obvious at first glance. For soldiers, they can be seen as symbols of luck and relief at having survived such an inhuman conflict and as objects which recall memories of comrades who shared these experiences but who did not return from the war. For the bereaved, such objects could represent feelings of grief, loss and mourning, as embodiments of equally cherished memories of loved ones who never came back and who lay in 'some corner of a foreign field'. Some pieces were poignantly associated with the landscapes of conflict and memorials through their role as souvenirs acquired on trips to the battlefields at any time from 1919 to the present. In each case, as we shall see, different kinds of Trench Art played different roles in stimulating a variety of emotions in the beholder.

In terms of modern scholarship, whether history, anthropology, archaeology or art history, Trench Art is increasingly being connected with issues of heritage. Museums, in particular, mount exhibitions whose displays focus ever more on the experiences of war of the ordinary soldier, prisoners of war and civilian refugees. In other words, quite apart from the visual attractiveness and often technical virtuosity of individual pieces, Trench Art can be seen as representing the intense relationships between human beings and the things they make and value during wartime and afterwards. Some of the qualities attached to Trench Art relate to human emotions of love, hate, fear and grief, as well as boredom, inventiveness and commercial advantage. The connections between these objects and the human feelings which they can invoke are a clear indication of the important role of Trench Art in trying to understand the experiences of all those who took part in or were otherwise affected by the Great War.

Trench Art is also a distinctive, attention-grabbing kind of artistic endeavour. Great War art has usually referred to paintings and drawings and to the monuments and memorial architecture which was erected during the post-war years. The graphic depictions of war painted by Paul Nash and Christopher Nevinson, amongst others, and monuments such as London's Cenotaph, and the memorials to 'The Missing' at Thiepval on the Somme, and Tyne Cot and the Menin Gate at Ieper (Ypres) in Flanders, are all representations of war at a distance – in time and space. At the time, artists and architects struggled to create ideas and forms which could represent the grim, anti-human forces unleashed by the war and which had appeared impossible to capture by old pre-war artistic and architectural conventions.

However, where paintings and memorials represented the war at arms length, much Trench Art, especially of metal, was made from the waste of war itself. Its strange and different shapes incorporated the agents of death and mutilation directly. Responsible for untold suffering and bereavement, expended shells, bullets and shrapnel were worked into many forms, engaging the senses of sight, sound, smell and touch in ways which were impossible for paintings and only marginally less so for memorials. In addition, Trench Art objects were small, portable, and could be bought by battlefield pilgrims and visitors to represent their own varied responses to the war and in light of their personal loss. Many such items were bought as souvenirs and taken home. During the inter-war years many of these objects became almost substitute husbands, sons and brothers to the bereaved, in a way which resonated with personal lives and private time. Great War memorials and fine art played a different and very public role in coming to terms with the war.

Trench Art can be seen as a universe containing many worlds of meaning. Some of these worlds are common and everyday, some are uniquely connected to traumatic events, while others relate to death, memory, and the human penchant for collecting souvenirs. These are the basic ideas which lie behind the confusing mass of different kinds of Trench Art. Before they can be explored we need to get to grips with the basics, to understand how these objects were made, by whom, and under what circumstances.

Fig. 1.1: Trench Art of a different kind. French photograph of an artist, his imaginative painting, and his subject in a presumably quiet sector.

Chapter 2

TRENCH ART, A CLASSIFICATION

The quantity and variety of Trench Art has hitherto discouraged any serious attempts to analyse or classify it. Previous publications have tended to be small articles written by enthusiasts and collectors and to have focused on a particularly unusual item or an especially impressive personal collection. At militaria fairs, auctions rooms and on the Internet, decorated shell cases, letter-openers, cigarette lighters and a host of other items from many different wars are usually briefly described and given arbitrary commercial values. Today, Trench Art is still seen as an ill-defined mass of curios relating to war – especially the Great War.

The absence of any classification – any way of making sense of diversity – means that Trench Art has no definite place in the world of antiques and collectables, still less has its historical and cultural significance been recognized. Consequently, it has been, and continues to be, regarded and sold under a variety of headings – as militaria, antiques, bric-a-brac, unusual museum pieces, souvenirs, mementoes and curios. Trench Art seems to exist in limbo as anonymous objects without ties or associations to the people who made or used it, or to the tumultuous times in which they lived.

Since the Second World War, it appears that Trench Art's quantity, variety and status as ephemera made and sold by ordinary soldiers, has relegated it to a lowly status hardly worthy of mention let alone study. Not only has its amorphous nature been seen as making any attempt to organize it a fruitless exercise, but in any case it has been widely judged to have no historical relevance. Such a view could not be further from the truth.

It is possible to identify a number of types of Trench Art, to date them, to describe different processes of manufacture and decoration, to identify some of the makers, and tentatively to assign meanings and associations to many of their shapes and forms. This is possible partly because Trench Art's variety is seen by anthropology not as a problem but an advantage. In other words, the variability of the objects tells of the social forces which created them. Together with memorials, cenotaphs, war cemeteries and remembrance ceremonies, Trench Art objects helped create a post-war world of memories and associations. A war orphan would regard 'Daddy's shell' in quite a different way than a surviving soldier, a bereaved widow, or the returning refugees who made them in vast quantities along the old Western Front, and elsewhere, between 1919 and 1939.

Although a focus on the objects and the circumstances of their manufacture can reveal much that has been hidden about Trench Art, it would be misleading to assume that it is possible to identify or classify every kind of object. There is just too much variety to be able to fit all items into neat categories – indeed this feature of Trench Art is an integral part of its attraction and significance. It is a common experience to those who collect or deal in this material to encounter a new piece, the like of which they have never seen before. Unexpected, sometimes spectacular, and probably one-off objects are part of the fascination of Trench Art.

A more intractable problem is a degree of overlap, where the same objects can appear in several different categories. The ubiquitous metal matchbox cover is an example. Many appear virtually identical, but in fact could have been made by front line soldiers, service personnel behind the lines, prisoners of war and by local civilians both during and after the war. Each had the same function, but according to who made it and when, each may possess a different significance. Only by attempting a classification can we begin to unravel the intricate histories of different kinds of what appear to be an identical group of objects.

This matchbox cover example illustrates the problems associated with interpreting Trench Art, partly explains why previous attempts have foundered, and also demonstrates how anthropology (and common sense) can squeeze information from the most unpromising material. More importantly, it underpins my approach to the classification developed below. This scheme organizes Trench Art not by grouping together the same objects or forms – which would lead to little more than an inventory of, say, all matchbox covers, all decorated shells, or all carved-wood items – but rather according to who made them, when and where. It is these three criteria which open the door to establishing the historical significance of Trench Art.

The initial classification which follows is based on a broad and representative number of examples found in museums, private collections, and militaria fairs around the world. The aim is not to make a once and for all judgement of how Trench Art should be classified or valued, either historically or commercially. Rather, it is hopeed that this provisional organization of the artefacts begins a process of ending the isolation of Trench Art by bringing its astonishing variety of shapes and forms into the wider world of artistic endeavour and appreciation. More especially, it is hoped that by revealing its human and cultural dimensions, to allow for the recognition of, and sensitivity towards, an unacknowledged aspect of the Great War. However imperfect and preliminary these categories may appear, hopefully they will go some way to reveal Trench Art for what it once was and what it has become.

CATEGORIES OF TRENCH ART

CATEGORY 1: Soldiers, 1914-1919

Trench Art made by soldiers, in the front line, behind the lines, in prisoner of war camps or recuperating in hospitals, is, perhaps surprisingly, the smallest category numerically speaking. This is due mainly to the fact that, despite the large numbers of men involved, its manufacture was restricted to some five years – just over four of war and just under one for the twin processes of prisoner repatriation and soldier demobilization (on all sides). Nevertheless, this category displays the greatest variety of forms, of which perhaps fifty percent were functional in nature.

This category is bounded by the dates 1914-1919, and by the identification of its makers as service personnel. However, there exists a qualitative difference between Trench Art made by soldiers on active service, that made by those who had become prisoners of war, and items made as therapy by soldiers recovering from wounds. For this reason, category 1 is sub-divided 1a, 1b, and 1c accordingly. The differences between these three sub-categories lay sometimes in the kinds of objects made, but more often in the materials available, the conditions under which they were made and the resonances which each had for its makers.

The overall inventiveness of category 1 pieces is illustrated by the variety of items listed below – some of which inevitably found parallels in objects produced by the makers of other categories.

Typical examples of category 1 items include:

i Smoking equipment: cigarette lighters made from bullets and/or scrap metal, matchbox covers commonly made from brass or steel scrap and often simply inscribed and decorated, tobacco boxes (of metal and/or wood), and tobacco cloth pouches, cigarette cases and ashtrays made from metal.

ii Writing equipment: letter-openers made from bullets and scrap metal, sometimes inscribed, and often with badges attached, pens/pencils made from defused bullets and cartridges, 'writing sets' made from scrap metals and often decorated with bullet/cartridges.

iii Artillery shell cases, simply decorated in or near the front lines by ordinary soldiers, or more elaborately shaped and decorated by service personnel behind the lines. Inscriptions sometimes appear to date a piece exactly, such as 'Ypres, 1914,1915,1916', though this is not always reliable.

iv Personal adornment: finger rings made mainly from aluminium, steel or brass, lockets and brooches made from scrap metal and sometimes incorporating defused bullets or cartridges, bracelets and wrist bands made from scrap metals and especially from ridged copper drive-bands, photograph frames made usually from scrap metal sometimes with a bullet/cartridge framing, and occasionally of exotic materials, such as Army Issue biscuits.

v Miniatures: tanks and aeroplanes made from scrap metals, military caps made from the base of a brass shell case, ships made from wood often said to come from a named vessel. Some of the above were made to function as money boxes.

vi Miscellaneous carved-wood objects, such as walking sticks, letter-holders and photograph frames.

vii Miscellaneous objects carved from bone, stone and chalk, often inscribed or decorated with a soldier's unit insignia and details, or the name of a POW camp.

viii Miscellaneous embroidered and beaded objects, such as decorated postcards, handkerchiefs, regimental insignia and heart-shaped decorative cushions.

ix Miscellaneous personal items decorated with, or made from, bullets, cartridges, shell fragments and assorted scrap metals, such as identity tags.

Sub-category 1a: Active service

Many soldiers carved in chalk, wood or bone in the trenches, but conditions under fire and the lack of appropriate tools were always thought to have precluded the manufacture of anything other than the crudest objects, particularly when it came to working metal. This remains a common assumption, though the truth is far more interesting.

We now know that many sophisticated items were made in these terrible conditions, and 'in view of the enemy'. Early on in the war, along the banks of the River Ijzer (Yser), French and Belgian soldiers made often elaborate finger rings from the aluminium fuzes and washers taken from incoming German shells. These were melted down and poured into a mould, filed, engraved and polished, and then sold or bartered to other soldiers or sent home to loved ones. British soldiers engaged in similar activities. In the Liddle Collection of Leeds University is a letter written by J. Laws in which he tells of how 'The lads in the trenches while away the flat time by fashioning rings, crosses, and pendants out of bullets and the softer parts of shells.'

Even though it can be shown that front line soldiers could and did

Fig. 2.1: Belgian soldiers making finger rings on the Ijzer (Yser) front, Belgium.

Courtesy of Roger Lampaert.

make occasionally impressive, though usually rather plain, pieces of Trench Art, it is nevertheless true that the majority of items belonging to this category were made behind the lines. In safer rear areas, off duty soldiers, blacksmiths, Royal Engineers, and service personnel of various units – including the Royal Flying Corps – all had the opportunity and incentive to make Trench Art. Spare time, boredom and the opportunity to supplement meagre wages was a powerful combination. There was also an international variety of skills and ingenuities at hand. According to Angela Kelsall, the Chinese Labour Corps made it their business to find out which regiments were in the area, proceeded to acquire the appropriate badges and buttons which they then used to decorate Trench Art items which were sold as souvenirs to these same regiments.

Fig. 2.3: Chinese lettering on an artillery shell case.

Fig. 2.4: Chinese dragon figure made from Arras clay with Chinese lettering.

Author copyright and acknowledgement to the Imperial War Museum

Many items in this category were functional (in the widest sense), and many were made 'on spec'. Others however were made to order, often engraved with a man's name, occasionally rank and regiment and sometimes also with a date or place name. As Jane Peek has pointed out, this personalization of objects led many relatives to mistakenly attribute the manufacture of a piece of Trench Art directly to a grandfather or uncle. Grandad's bullet-lighter or matchbox cover might have been made by him, but equally could have been a commissioned piece paid for with a few cigarettes or a couple of beers when out of the line.

It is clear that the majority of examples in this category were made by individuals who had the time, expertise, incentive, and safe location to engage in such activities. While wood, bone, chalk or embroidery required only the simplest of implements and raw materials, in the case of metals, access to tools to cut, shape, weld, solder, engrave and polish were somewhat more difficult to come by. All these objects had a value, either as a personal memento, or by virtue of being bartered, sold or sent home to family and friends as souvenirs.

Sub-category 1b: Prisoner of War

Soldiers on all sides who had been captured also produced Trench Art of various kinds. However, the materials available and the conditions under which they were made were quite different from those of sub-category 1a. Prisoners of war were no longer in conflict

Fig. 2.4: French soldiers dealing in Trench Art and other souvenirs.

Fig. 2.9: Allied prisoners making wooden boxes and photograph frames at Dülmen PoW camp, Germany.

situations, their lives were not at risk from enemy action and conditions, generally speaking, were considerably more agreeable than life in the trenches. Hardship nevertheless attended such a status, and one way in which prisoners could alleviate boredom, earn extra money, food and favours, was by making things to sell and trade. To call such objects 'Prisoner of War Art' is not inaccurate, yet it does not get us far. As such objects were clearly related to war, were made by men who probably also had previously made or acquired category 1a items, and may well be involved with category 3 items (see below), there seems little point in separating them out as a somehow entirely different kind of endeavour.

In prisoner of war camps, Trench Art objects were made primarily of wood, bone and textiles. The scrap metals associated with battlefields were not generally available, though bully beef tins could substitute on many occasions, and occasionally brass and copper were available. The difference in materials led to different kinds of objects being made, and to the associations of these objects differing from those in category 1a.

A degree of confusion surrounds category 1b items just as it does other kinds of Trench Art. Objects were made by prisoners not just for themselves or each other but also to sell to, or exchange with, their captors. Thus, a carved wooden cigarette box with the monogram 'Capt. L. Mills, KOYLI, Lens 1919', was made for him by a German prisoner of war – a fact only available to us because documentary evidence has survived. In the Middle East, Turkish prisoners of war made unusual items, such as a miniature pair of boots made from white China clay and exchanged for water. More common were the striking 'beadwork snakes', sometimes with lettering picked out in black beads and saying, for example, 'Turkish Prisoner 1915'. These

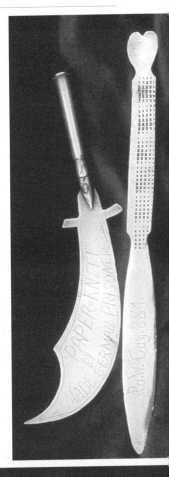

Fig. 2.6: PoW metal letter openers.

Fig. 2.7: Beadwork snake, made by a Turkish PoW.

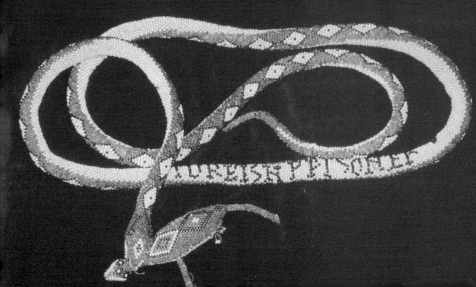

beady serpents are themselves an ambiguous kind of Trench Art, for they appear, virtually identical, in a quite different category, 2c, which is documented below.

Sub-category 1c: The Wounded

The First World War produced maimed and wounded in large numbers. Apart from those who had sustained physical injury, there were those who suffered from a new kind of affliction – shell shock. In both cases, the medical authorities considered that each recovering soldier should undertake therapeutic exercise as and where appropriate. This meant that many soldiers, wounded in action, were encouraged to make things primarily towards their own recovery, but also to help raise money for themselves and others.

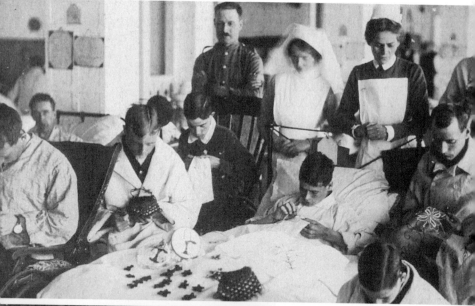

Fig. 2.8: Recuperating British soldiers making embroideries.

Fig. 2.9: Heart-shaped decorative cushion.

According to the kind of injury sustained, wounded servicemen would make items from wood, such as picture frames and boxes, and a variety of embroideries and textiles, of which the most typical and popular were the heart-shaped decorative cushions. These were often brightly coloured, sometimes decorated with beads and/or embroidery and occasionally also with photographs. Although perhaps the majority of the wounded recovered quickly and were certainly discharged by 1919, a significant number lingered on in hospitals and rest homes for many years, continuing to make these and other items.

One ironic example stands out here and involves St. Dunstan's Hospital in London, which cared for soldiers blinded during the war. When it was decided to replace the temporary cenotaph in London's Whitehall with a permanent version, the wood used in the original plaster construction was given to St. Dunstan's, with the intention of encouraging the inmates to make photograph frames. Such was the (unexpected) public demand for images of the cenotaph, however, that

Fig. 2.10: British soldier operating a treadle to exercise his foot.

the blinded soldiers were requested to use the wood instead to make bases for miniature bronze models of the cenotaph which were then offered for sale on 20 April 1920. It is debateable whether or not this qualifies as Trench Art. Therapy is one thing, profit another. Yet these men had been blinded by the war and both the objects themselves and their makers, were poignantly connected to the war's terrible consequences.

With the exception of these and similar items within sub-category 1c, all kinds of category 1 Trench Art ceased to be made in the period between the Armistice of 11 November 1918 and the signing of the Peace Treaty of Versailles in July 1919, during which time prisoners of war were released, and the majority of active servicemen demobilized and returned home.

Nevertheless, many servicemen stayed on until September or October of 1919, and a considerable number subsequently became the forces of occupation on the Rhine. These continued to make Trench Art of various kinds mainly as souvenirs, such as two remarkable privately owned carved wood plaques, one inscribed 'Souvenir of Alsace Lorraine, December 1918-20', the other 'Souvenir from Germany, December 1918-20'. In all probability, this was a relatively short-lived phenomenon but would bear future investigation.

CATEGORY 2: Civilians, 1914-1939

The war had a terrible effect on civilian life, especially along the Western Front in France and Belgium, and on the Eastern Front. Economic deprivation, the destruction of towns and farms, and the incredible quantities of available war matériel strewn over the land combined to produce the conditions for a thriving civilian industry in Trench Art. This lasted for twenty-five years from 1914 to 1939. As a result, category 2, which can be sub-divided into 2a, 2b and 2c, was by far the largest in terms of the overall quantity of items produced. The variety of shapes was less than category 1 and items tended towards the ornamental rather than the functional. They were also less often made to order and consequently far less personalized.

The differences between sub-categories 2a and 2b are significant and informative, yet at the same time often difficult to establish. In both cases, identical forms often were made by the same people working the same materials with the same tools and techniques. Except where a piece was dated, or had an inscription which indicated the war was over, the difference between the two categories lay not in materials or shapes, but in the changing circumstances of manufacture and sale associated with the move from war to peace. The resonances of these apparently identical pieces were also different, as 2a items were sold mainly to soldiers during the war, while 2b objects were sold to war widows, pilgrims and battlefield tourists between 1919 and 1939.

Sub-category 2c was also made by civilians displaced by war, but not directly associated with the battlefields. These were civilians resident in the enemy's country at the outbreak of hostilities, and who had been incarcerated in internment camps. Although there are obvious links to sub-category 1b, i.e. POWs, the differences are such that sub-category 2c objects can most usefully be considered under a civilian rather than soldier heading.

Typical examples of category 2 items include:

i   Smoking equipment: matchbox covers commonly made from brass scrap and often bearing an inscription and date which implies a finished war, and ashtrays usually made from scrap brass and sometimes decorated with bullet cartridges. These frequently bear dates and inscriptions indicating post-war manufacture, and sometimes have small, commercially made 'memorial plaques' attached, depicting, for example, the Menin Gate at Ieper (Ypres) (i.e. 1927). They are generally more elaborate than category 1 examples.

ii Writing equipment: letter-openers made from bullets and scrap metal, sometimes with badges attached, and almost always with the blade decorated with a design incorporating an inscription such as 'Souvenir of the Great War, 1914-1918', pens/pencils made from defused bullets and cartridges, and 'writing sets' made from scrap metals and often decorated with bullet/cartridges – these can be exquisitely made – the degree of sophistication and the presence of a 'memorial plaque' differentiating them from category 1 examples.

iii Artillery shell cases, usually of brass, sometimes elaborately shaped (e.g. with 'corsetted' or fluted lower sections), often decorated with generic art nouveau floral designs, and frequently engraved with the name of a town and/or region, a date, and such archetypal post-war inscriptions as 'Souvenir of the World War 1914-1918'. Smaller calibre shell cases were also made, decorated with a memorial plaque and sometimes mounted on a tripod of bullets.

iv Bullet-crucifixes made of bullets and their cartridges, often with a commercially produced Christ figure, regimental badge or memorial plaque attached. These are invariably mounted on a tripod of bullets which can be of any nationality. While bullet-crucifixes were made also during the war (they have been found on battlefields), the majority appear to have been made during

the inter-war years.
v   Miscellaneous metal objects, usually made for the home, such as serviette rings made from shell and fuze parts, and often indistinguishable from category 1, unless dated.
vi Miscellaneous carved wooden objects, such as walking sticks, letter-holders and photograph frames, usually identified by a post-war date.
vii Miscellaneous bone objects, such as flower vases carved from the leg bones of horses or oxen.
viii Miscellaneous embroidered objects, such as decorated postcards, handkerchiefs, tablecloths, laces and painted linens showing, for example, the burning of the Cloth Hall at Ieper (Ypres), and the leaning Golden Madonna and Child atop the Basilica at Albert. Many of these also have embroidered/painted inscriptions of post-war date, and with the words 'Souvenir of the Great War 1914-1918' applied.

Sub-category 2a: 1914-1918

In a war-ravaged economy, civilian manufacture of Trench Art – especially of metals – quickly became a cottage industry. The Allied and German armies were a large, albeit shifting, market for such items. Although many civilians found themselves caught on different sides of the front line, this did not adversely affect their Trench Art making activities. Locally made embroideries, carved wooden items and especially metal objects, were sold and traded to all soldiers irrespective of nationality. Metal matchbox covers vividly illustrate the point: examples exist which depict the typical German spiked helmet (pickelhaube) on

Fig. 2.11: Metal matchbox cover decorated with 'Gott Mit Uns' (God With Us).

Fig. 2.12: French civilians collecting unfired artillery shells..

one side, an inscription 'Gott mits uns' (God with us) on the other, and 'Fabrique en France' along the spine.

Sub-category 2b: 1919-1939

For civilians, the harsh economic conditions of the war continued after the Armistice. Towns and cities were devastated, and a primarily agricultural landscape rendered useless and dangerous by four years of saturation shelling and vast quantities of unexploded ordnance. In the Ypres Salient, up to five unexploded artillery shells could be found in one square metre, and some 5000 kilos of shrapnel and detonators per hectare. Collecting and neutralizing this was a huge and risky undertaking which, in a very real sense, has still not been completed. Often, the young children of returning refugees were sent out into the killing fields to collect scrap metal as a way of earning money for the

Fig. 2.13: Pair of Trench Art Souvenir shells mounted on a tripod of bullets. The memorial plaque shows the Menin gate at Ieper (Ypres) and thus dates the piece from 1927 onwards.

Fig. 2.14: Richard Dezitter, a well known Trench Art maker from inter-war Ieper (Ypres) with an example of his handiwork.

family – who either sold it on or used it to make Trench Art souvenirs. Sometimes these children never returned. In any event, the gathering of the debris of war created huge stockpiles of metals. Yet, while there was an ever increasing amount of available raw materials with which to make metal Trench Art, there was a correspondingly rapid decrease of soldiers and service personnel around to buy it.

Between 1919 and 1939 however, a new market for such items appeared in the large numbers of pilgrims and tourists visiting the battlefields and the associated cemeteries and memorials being constructed by the Imperial War Graves Commission (now the

Commonwealth War Graves Commission). Those who once made and sold Trench Art to Allied soldiers now sold often identical items to the bereaved widows, sweethearts and relatives of those who had not returned from the war. Tragically ironic was that some of the war widows must have bought Trench Art souvenirs fashioned from the very shells and bullets which they themselves had produced in munitions factories during the war.

The manufacture and sale of sub-category 2b items ended in 1939 when the flow of pilgrims and visitors ended abruptly with the advent of the Second World War. This conflict produced its own kinds of Trench Art but these are beyond the scope of the present book.

Sub-category 2c: 1914-1919

Forcibly placed in various camps throughout Europe, civilian internees also made countless objects which can be considered Trench Art. There is little reason to complicate matters unnecessarily by creating a new category of 'Internment Camp Art'. Although the internees, in Britain at least, had not taken up arms to fight, their status was a result of war, and their conditions, and the objects they made, were often indistinguishable from those made by prisoners of war. However, the resonances associated with making such objects could

Fig. 2.15: Display of arts and crafts made by the internees at Knockaloe Camp, Isle of Man.   *Courtesy of Manx National Heritage.*

never be the same for a civilian as for a soldier who had seen the face of battle.

The work of Yvonne Cresswell of the Manx Museum has chronicled the lives and experiences of men interned on the Isle of Man, providing a rich insight into their 'leisure time' activities. With makeshift machinery, time and ingenuity, the Germans, Austrians and Turks who found themselves imprisoned, made inlaid wooden boxes, marquetry pictures and miscellaneous wooden trinkets for barter and sale. In particular, the remains of the large numbers of animals consumed in the camps were put to good use. Countless art nouveau style flower vases, ashtrays, letter-openers, and brooches were made from the leg bones of animals. Apart from the inscriptions, these were often identical to items produced in POW camps. The acute shortage of industrial strength metals was made up for by the ready supply of bully beef tins which were cut and flattened into sheets as raw material for making mugs, candlesticks and ashtrays.

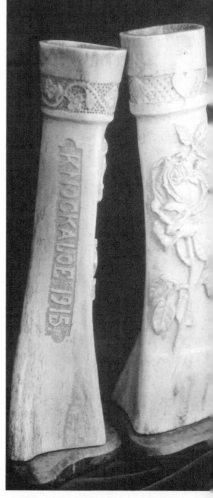

Fig. 2.16: Carved ox bone vases made by the internees of Knockaloe Camp, Isle of Man.

The work of Turkish internees highlights the often intractable problem of differentiating between the work of military POWs and civilian internees. Their beadwork snakes were so similar to those made by their compatriots who languished as POWs in the Middle East that even today bead experts are surprised to learn that they were not made only in POW camps or solely in internment camps.

Sub-category 2c objects may seem to strain common assumptions of where the boundaries of Trench Art should lay. Yet, as with sub-category 1c, these items clearly fall within my working definition. Being interned was a consequence of the war and many of the objects made in internment camps embodied feelings of boredom, depression, estrangement and also artistic creativity – the less deadly civilian equivalent of the emotions represented by Trench Art made by soldiers, POWs, the wounded and displaced civilians in battlefield areas.

The making of 2c items ended between 1918 and 1919, during which time most internees were returned, not to the British addresses from where they had been taken, but to their country of origin. Some had married British girls before the war and now faced permanent separation and divorce as their wives often would not accompany them. For these, the objects they had made while interned, and had kept for themselves, must have had bitter-sweet connotations.

CATEGORY 3: c.1918-c.1939

The third category of Trench Art considered here is arguably the most clearly defined of all, in terms of its distinctive forms, the places and circumstances of manufacture and often the specific names of its makers. Paradoxically, it has so far not been possible to assign other than general dates to the period during which it was made. Category 3 items were made in Britain, though possibly elsewhere also, towards the end of the war, but mainly after the Armistice. These objects were fashioned from the 'raw', unworked, and often randomly collected materials of war brought back as miscellaneous mementoes and souvenirs by returning soldiers.

The transformation of these odd items of war matériel into cultural objects was undertaken commercially by various British firms, large and small, and one of which, the Army and Navy Store, produced the advertisement shown here. The organized commercial nature of this undertaking contrasted with the ad hoc cottage industry production of category 2. Where the latter contributed piecemeal to local economies, the profits of category 3 often went straight to established companies which had already done well from four and a half years of war.

The service offered by these firms was to personalize soldier's souvenirs and memorabilia by creating often sophisticated and distinctive designs, and mounting them typically on a black ebonized

712

No. 8, TAXIDERMY—No. 3, Howick Place.

Deptl. Enquiry Telephone

GUN & SPORTING DEPARTMENT (Naturalist Section).

MEMBERS' OWN

WAR TROPHIES MOUNTED

To any design.   Estimates and designs submitted.

The illustrations are of Trophies which have been mounted by the Society for Members.

The prices quoted are approximate and are published for members' guidance. It will be well, however, to avoid any misunderstanding, that members should have an official estimate given before any trophy is proceeded with.

NOTICE.—The Society cannot undertake the responsibility of unloading shells or cartridges, and all such trophies must be unloaded before delivery, failing which they will at once be returned to the sender.

OLD ARMS, ARMOUR, &c., as TROPHIES.—The Society undertakes the cleaning and mounting, on shields, &c., of all kinds of old Arms, Armour, and Military Trophies of every description. Sketches and estimates submitted.

Shell Case as Gong, on stand............£3 2s.

Shell Case, Mounted on Two Bayonets as Gong .... £2 0s. 0d.

Shell Head as Letter Weight 10/6
Shell Head as Inkstand, on ebonized base 25/0
Shell Head as Match Stand on ebonized base 22/6

Grenade as Candlestick and Match Holder...40/0

Shell as Clock ... £5 4s. 0d.

Shells as Table Lamp, metal, base, electro-plate, polished brass, copper or iron......50/0

Shell Case as Flower Stand, ebonized plinth, in polished brass, 20/0

Shell Case as on oak back.

Shell Head as Letter Clip, on ebonized base 23/0

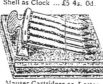

Mauser Cartridges as Letter Weight and Clip, 21/0

Fragment of Shell, on ebonized base ... 3

Part of Shell, on ebonized base ...., 20/0

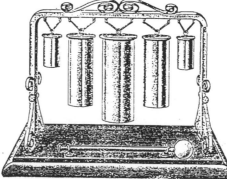

5 Shell Cases as Table Gong, on ebonized plinth ....£6 2s. 0d.

Base of Shell Inkstand

PRICES SUBJECT TO ALTERATION WITHOUT NOTICE.

Fig. 2.17: Army and Navy Store advertisement for the mounting of war trophies.

base. It was this distinctive black base which unified the diversity of items, from a simple shrapnel fragment to an elaborate clock or table lamp. In general, these items were often more elaborate than any previous category. Mounted, and thereby 'civilized', they were often referred to as 'Mounted War Trophies', and appear to have owed much to the pre-1914 British imperial traditions of displaying shields and spears, rifles, lions heads and tiger skins as trophies from encounters in the far-flung corners of empire.

Typical examples of category 3 items include:

i   Clocks made from artillery shell cases and bullets, or commercially made and mounted on artillery shells or shell cases.

ii   Lamps and candlesticks made from artillery shell cases and grenades, and sometimes decorated with bullets.

iii Inkwells and elaborate 'writing sets' made from grenades, and/or artillery shell fuzes and/or shrapnel fragments.

iv   Mounted but otherwise unmodified objects, such as artillery shell fuzes, shrapnel fragments, shell or bullet parts as ornaments or paperweights.

v   Various size 'cups' made from artillery shell case parts and often with simple spiral handles or adornments.

vi   'Table gongs' of various sizes and degrees of elaboration, made from artillery shell cases.

Almost all these items were designed for the home and the peacetime lives of returning soldiers. Because of this it is difficult to establish their emotional importance. Some items may have possessed a strong emotional resonance, e.g. a bullet or piece of shrapnel which had wounded but not killed – a mounted reminder of an all too close brush with eternity. On the other hand, an object may have been picked up on the battlefield as a memento with no special significance.

More generally, these items served to civilize or tame the experience of war, to soften harsh memories and to embody the 'swords into ploughshares' philosophy – a phrase sometimes engraved on these objects. In all probability, many served as visual reminders of wartime experiences – either as collective talking points, or, more likely – given the well known reticence of Great War soldiers to talk of their experiences – as private memories. It seems probable that by their nature, category 3 items predominated in homes where the menfolk had survived, in contrast perhaps to sub-category 2b, whose objects were more likely found among families which had suffered the loss of a father, brother or son.

This classification is, as already stated, a first attempt to bring some kind of order to a seemingly chaotic mass of objects. Despite its preliminary nature, it has revealed the scale of the undertaking, and how the problems of categorization can suggest different ways of looking at and investigating these objects. To follow up this classification in every respect is beyond the scope of the present book. What follows, therefore, is a broad assessment of the main kinds of Trench Art based on the materials used to make them, and including examples made by soldiers, civilians and prisoners of war.

Fig. 2.18: Post-war shell-clock made by Belgian metalsmith with art nouveau decoration and 'Dixmude' engraved around the base.

Fig. 2.19: Post-war corsetted shell-lamp.

Chapter 3

THE ART OF SHELLS

Big, dazzling and covered with striking artistic motifs, the decorated artillery shell case is the archetypal Trench Art object. Yet, as we have seen, such icons of industrialized war are of different kinds, with the majority of the elaborate examples belonging to the inter-war years.

These objects, by their size and variety, can yield important information about the maker's expertise, or lack of it, and indicate the kinds of tools which were used. Equally interesting is that by their sheer numbers and diversity, they carry information on the artistic styles used to adorn them and, more widely, the symbolic resonances of the cultural and personal forces at work in their production. There is little doubt that, as the defining weapon of the First World War, artillery shells were, at one and the same time, symbols of modernism often decorated in a romantic art nouveau style which derived from a world which the war itself was working overtime to destroy.

Fig. 3.1: Fine example of Trench Art brass artillery shell case, decorated with copper, a regimental badge, and bullets, and serving as a money box.

The Birth of the Shell

The origin of the decorated artillery shell case is surrounded by irony and poignancy. In order to explore the full range of meanings which these objects had for those who made and used them we need to start at the beginning, with the creation of the raw material itself, i.e. the manufacturing of shells in munitions factories. While in military terms the loaded shell was the finished item, from the perspective of Trench Art it was the initial stage of production, the forging of objects from which decorated pieces would later be made.

For the British, although the conflict had begun as a man's war in the Victorian tradition of heroic acts admired from afar by womenfolk, its nature quickly changed. In the wake of early military setbacks and attrition, which destroyed Britain's small professional army and quickened the consequent recruitment of Kitchener's Army, the country was increasingly depleted of young men. Women were expected to 'do their bit' by taking over many industrial jobs. The metal trades, which included fuze and cartridge making, saw an increase of some 424,000 women between 1914 and 1918. At Woolwich Arsenal, for example, there were 400 women employed in 1915, but by the time of the armistice this had increased to 27,000. Already by 1916, Boyd Cable wrote that the whole country was one 'seething munition factory', and, by war's end, Winston Churchill commented that the British Isles had become an arsenal.

Fig. 3.2: Women employed in making shells in a wartime munitions factory.

At the beginning of the war, Edwardian society regarded women as the peaceful nurturers of the British race. Soon, in an irony not lost on many, there was an inversion of this traditional role whereby women became primary arms producers, furnishing men with the weapons of mass destruction. The ironies are striking. Working in munitions factories was not simply a way for around a million women to help their absent menfolk – it also fundamentally changed their views on life in what, to that point, had been a man's world of work.

For women, a job in a munitions factory represented a unique opportunity to escape often claustrophobic and badly paid service 'below stairs' and enter a comparatively well-paid atmosphere of factory work. Some 400,000 women left domestic service mainly for munitions and transport work between 1914 and 1918 – a fact which began to erode the male-centred notion of civilization for which the war, at least in part, was being fought. Munitions work offered British women financial independence and a feeling of autonomy and liberation.

Yet this was achieved at the price of producing bullets, guns and bombs which had exactly the opposite effect for soldiers on the front line. As women emerged from 'below stairs' up into the well-lit world of factory work, men descended into the dark and dangerous world of trenches and dugouts, forced to take shelter from the enemy barrage of shells made by other women. British munitionettes often saw their work in soldierly terms. Mrs Alec-Tweedie relates a conversation between a parlourmaid and her fiancé who was about to leave for France – 'While you are at the front firing shells, I am going into a munition factory to make shells ... and every time you fire your gun you can remember I am helping to make the shells.' Not all women felt the same way. Some were only too conscious of the fact that they were working to destroy other peoples' loved ones and that all their efforts were concentrated on bringing misery and death to other young men.

The industrialization of armament manufacture produced greater quantities of arms than ever before, and yielded an increase in numbers of dead and maimed in equally industrial numbers. In this sense, the battlefield was like a continuation of the factory. In some ways, even before shells arrived at the front they already had a story to tell as symbolic objects of women's changing roles. The social aspects of Trench Art shell cases began with the birth of the shell.

Fig. 3.3 a,b,c: Artillery shells with messages chalked on for those on the receiving end (not that they would ever read them).

The Makers and their Techniques

Artillery shells arrived at the front packed in cases and sometimes accompanied by tender notes slipped in between them by munitionettes eager to boost Tommy's morale. Unloaded and stacked ready for use, and sometimes when already in the breech, gunners would anticipate later artistic endeavours by drawing a caricature of the Kaiser or a stereotyped 'Fritz' onto the cold metal. Often they would chalk an insult or worse. Thus, before the shell was fired, it was already carrying a message of sorts from one side to the other. However, it was after the shell had been sent on its way and the empty casing ejected hot and smoking onto the ground that the making of Trench Art began in earnest.

Artillery shell cases were made into Trench Art by a variety of people with different backgrounds and levels of skill and for many different reasons. On the Western Front at least, the wide variation in sophistication of these objects resulted from the equally wide differences in available skills. While some were made by soldiers who had never worked such things before, others were produced by consummate metalsmiths such as the Belgian copper workers from Antwerp who joined the Belgian Army at the beginning of the war. These individuals simply transferred their skills to working shells in the comparatively quiet area of the Ijzer (Yser) front north of Ieper (Ypres) where they were stationed.

There was also a range of varying skills available among French and Belgian civilians who, during and after the war, made vast quantities of such artefacts. Some were accomplished amateurs while others had competent metalworking or blacksmithing skills. As the differences between categories 1, 2a and 2b have already highlighted, somewhere between fifty and sixty percent of decorated shell cases were made by these civilians after 1918, during the twenty years of the inter-war period. As our classification also shows, what was previously regarded as a large undifferentiated group of shell case art can be broken down by the sophistication of manufacture and decoration which themselves, and quite apart from dated inscriptions, were often a marker of the different groups of people who made them.

The ordinary unskilled soldier in or near the front line did make such objects, despite the conditions he was living in, though the time spent in the trenches before an attack was comparatively small. One of the best documented examples of such a case are two decorated shell

Fig. 3.4: Decorated British 18 pounder shell case in art nouveau style and marked 'Souvenir of Loos'.

cases in London's Imperial War Museum. When they were donated they were accompanied by a letter in which their maker described how he had 'bought a transfer from a Belgian soldier for 5 Woodbines ... then transferred the design to the shell with a bent nail ...'. In this way he decorated two British 18-pounder shell cases with 'nouveau style female figures and flowers', one inscribed 'Souvenir of Loos', the other 'Souvenir of Ypres'. On returning home, he polished and lacquered them, keeping both on his mantelpiece for sixty years. There must have been countless similar cases, but the documentary evidence has either been lost or lies hidden away in boxes or in the reams of uncatalogued letters in museum storerooms.

By piecing together different kinds of evidence it is possible to recreate that scene. The transfer which is referred to as having been bought from a Belgian soldier is in fact a paper template. In a remarkable photograph in the Royal Army Museum, Brussels, three Belgian soldiers are shown making Trench Art

Fig. 3.5: Belgian soldiers decorating artillery shell cases, on the River Ijzer (Yser) north of Ieper (Ypres). *Courtesy of Roger Lampaert*

shell vases on the Ijzer (Yser) front. The soldier in the middle is working a shell case which has just such a template wrapped around it. With the paper secured by twine at both ends, he is following the design with a hammer and punch. Other soldiers simply drew their designs onto paper and glued this to the shell and then followed the design with their specially made tools, or tools which they had bought from local ironmongers. Some-times simple designs were drawn onto the shell, outlined in shallow punch-holes, with the holes then joined up by scoring as with children's dot-and-line drawings.

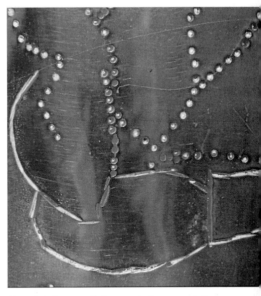

Fig. 3.6: Dot and line technique used in engraving an artillery shell.

As with the Belgian copper workers, there were other kinds of soldiers and service personnel who had a distinct advantage over those in the front line when it came to making Trench Art. These included mechanics, fitters, farriers, the Royal Engineers and others, such as the Chinese Labour Corps, all of whom had the skills, equipment, and opportunity to make often sophisticated Trench Art shell vases (as well as all kinds of other objects) in the relative safety of the rear areas.

Despite the variety of skills and motivations, the basic techniques for working shell cases were the same for everyone. First, an empty shell case had to be selected. This in itself was a contentious issue because, in the case of British shells at least, it was technically illegal for individuals to remove shell cases from the battlefield. They remained the property of the British government and were supposed to be collected into dumps, sorted and taken back to Britain to be refilled in munitions factories and then fired again at a later date. Brass was an expensive metal, and on the bottom of many shell cases are the tell-tale symbols which indicate how many times that particular shell case had been reused. Belgian soldiers too had to be cautious so as not to be reprimanded for stealing army property. One result of this was that most wartime pieces were not signed by their makers, but inscribed with the names of girlfriends or fiancées or the town in which they lived. In reality however, there were so many shell cases of every nationality laying around that obtaining such raw materials could never have been a problem.

Once a shell had been selected, the knowledgeable maker tested the structural integrity of the metal by flicking it with the finger and judging the resulting echo. The deeper and longer the sound the more likely it was that the shell's structure was intact and the less likely it was that an invisible flaw would later lead to the abandonment of a half-finished piece. Nevertheless, not all took this precaution. There are many examples where work had to be abandoned before the piece was finished due to a crack appearing in the shell, particularly in the

Fig. 3.7: Artillery shell case dump. It was technically illegal for soldiers to remove shell cases as brass was an expensive metal and the cases were to be returned to Britain for re-filling.

elaborate corsetted variety, where the individual flutes often pinched the metal extremely thin.

After a shell had been deemed suitable, the processes of decorating and sometimes shaping, the metal began. Trying to decorate an empty shell case was awkward if not impractical as there was nothing to hit against. Some kinds of decoration were so primitive that almost certainly they were applied in this most basic way. To overcome this problem and to produce something more aesthetically pleasing, several kinds of materials were inserted into the shell to provide the necessary resistance, against which the worker could hammer, punch and chisel his design.

At the beginning of the war, those not familiar with professional techniques would put a block of wood inside the shell, but this often proved difficult to extract and there is evidence that sometimes it had to be burnt out. This method was usually quickly abandoned. More frequent was the use of hot sand which softened (but did not melt) the metal, and could easily be emptied and reused. Sand was probably always available even to the front line soldier in the many sandbags used to reinforce the trenches. An alternative technique was to fill the shell case with bitumen which also warmed the metal and, when it had cooled, provided a solid but appropriately yielding resistance.

Possibly the most common, and arguably most effective technique, was the traditional method of pouring liquid lead into the shell. This also warmed the metal and, when it cooled, provided the best resistance against which elaborate designs could be worked into the metal. When the work was finished the shell was reheated and the lead poured out for reuse. Some enterprising soldiers melted down the lead balls found in shrapnel shells to serve as a matrix. More often it was probably the case that lead was not always available to the common soldier, and was easier to acquire for the likes of the Royal Engineers behind the lines.

A dramatic insight into this method is provided

Fig. 3.8: Unfinished artillery shell found near Ieper (Ypres) in 1999.
Author copyright with acknowledgement to the Association for Battlefield Archaeology, Flanders.

by a unique discovery in 1999 of an unfinished Trench Art shell vase in a field outside of Ieper (Ypres) in Belgium. This piece, a British 18-pounder, was only half finished when abandoned still with its lead matrix inside. The lower part had been completely shaped in the corsetted style, and the worker had just begun to incise designs into the upper part. As can be seen in the photograph, one advantage of using lead was the ability to include a handle in the matrix so as to be able to manoeuvre the heavy object more easily while working it. Such was the confusion of Great War battlefields with their shifting front lines, especially in the muddy Ypres Salient, that it is impossible to know whether this piece was begun and abandoned during the war or afterwards. A plausible but unprovable case could be made for either possibility.

Perhaps the most startling decorative technique was the corsetting or fluting of the lower half or third of the shell case. This could have

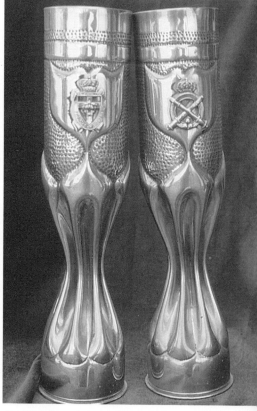

Fig. 3.9: Artillery shell case with rudimentary corsetting

Fig. 3.10: Pair of elaborately corsetted French 75mm artillery shell case.

been achieved in several ways. First, a specially shaped wooden punch could have been used to hammer against the warmed metal, with the sharp edges of each fluting filed down to prevent cracking. Section by section, over many hours, this would have produced the desired effect. While some efforts are so amateurish that it is almost certain that a wooden punch was used in an unskilled imitation of more masterly efforts, some of the finest pieces may possibly have been made in another way.

Some corsetted shell cases have their fluting perfectly symmetrical, suggesting the standardized spacings of a specially made vice-like tool which fitted around the lower part of the shell case and was then squeezed inwards. Occasionally, such corsetting was given an added artistic flourish by being twisted. It is difficult to see how these masterpieces of Trench Art could have been made by anyone other than specialists like the Belgian metalsmith soldiers, Royal Engineers or similar units within the Allied forces who had access to machine tools.

After the shaping, decorating and inscribing were finished, the shell case was reheated, the matrix extracted and the shell left to cool. It was then cleaned and polished and sometimes lacquered. The item was then ready to be sold, bartered or sent home as a souvenir.

Fig. 3.11: Corsetted and twisted French 75mm artillery shell case.

Styles, Stories, and Decoration

It is one of the ironies of metal Trench Art, and decorated shell cases in particular, that most were decorated with pastoral motifs such as flowers, leaves, and romanticized images of women typical of the art nouveau style which had flourished since the 1890s. Such neo-classical artistic ideals, incorporating roses, poppies and elegant branches adorned with thin leaves, probably appealed to many of those who felt moved to make such items. However, this artificially florid style, perhaps more a passing fashion of taste than of art, combined with the

Fig. 3.12: (above left) *Example of the art nouveau style of decoration.*

Fig. 3.13: (above right) *Pair of German shell cases decorated in art nouveau style with the Alsace-Lorraine cross motif.*

Fig. 3.14: (left) *Unusual art nouveau style with liquid lead dripped and shaped onto a British 18 pounder artillery shell case.*

Fig. 3.16: Pair of 77 mm shell case vases, decorated with the Flanders Lion motif and stamped 'Dinant'.

Fig. 3.15: 1915 German shell case with French soldier on guard duty holding rifle.

Fig. 3.17: Elaborately worked cases inscribed 'LC' and capped with spikes from German pickelhaube *helmets.*

Fig. 3.18: Base of a British 18 pounder shell made into a well.

Fig. 3.19: Intricate surface decoration on a shell case.

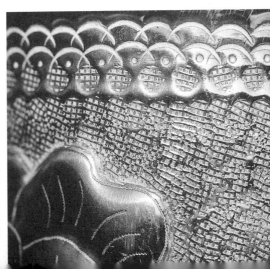

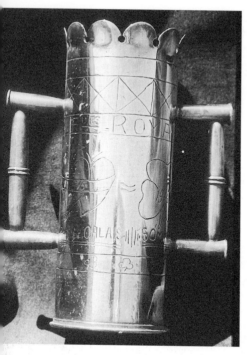

Fig. 3.20: French 75mm artillery shell case with handles made of Belgian bullets.

raw material of the shell to produce highly ambiguous artefacts. Definitively modern objects were shaped and covered with designs from a more innocent pre-war era.

The differing skills, motivations and backgrounds of those who made these objects nevertheless led to a variety of decoration and finish. Some are stunningly beautiful, while others show absolutely no artistic ability whatsoever – in fact sometimes appear childlike in their mix of naivety and imprecision. While from an art historical approach the former may be seen as valuable and the latter classed as little more than junk, from an anthropological perspective both are equally informative – indeed the diversity itself tells us much of value.

Many soldiers with no previous experience or skill in working metals (or any other raw materials) would make their own shell case vases, decorate them with their own idiosyncratic designs, and often engrave names of places, dates, and their own regimental details. A wonderful example of this is a French 75mm 1916 Trench Art shell case 'vase-with-handles', the latter made of four Belgian bullet cartridges, the top of the shell being crenellated, and the body inscribed in rustic style with 'Royal Inniskilling Furs', beneath which is a scroll with '1914' within it, a pair of hearts with '1915' inside, a three-leaf clover with '1916' within, and a poppy with '1917' inside. Beneath this is a longer inscription, 'Pas De Calais. Somme. Dunes'. A charming and authentic touch is the spelling of the name 'Belgiam'. This piece appears to have been decorated and inscribed, if not made and shaped, by an unskilled soldier certainly not before 1916, and possibly not after 1917.

Fig. 3.21: The Basilica at Albert on the Somme in 1999, together with a recent mural commemorating the leaning Golden Madonna and Child, and dated 1916.

The range of professionally made artillery shell case vases is equally striking. Many of these carry designs of landmarks well known to many soldiers at the time, such as the basilica at Albert on the Somme. One of the finest of these is in the Historial de la Grande Guerre (Péronne, France), and was produced in the months following the armistice. Made from a French 75mm shell case manufactured in 1916, it shows a superbly rendered image of the basilica with its famous leaning Golden Madonna and Child, which had been dislodged, appropriately, by a German shell on 15 January 1915. Along the bottom is an inscription which says, 'Basilique d'Albert, Guerre – 1914-19'. Similarly fine 'landmark' examples show the burning Cloth Hall

Fig. 3.22: French 75mm shell case, 1916, decorated with the Basilica at Albert and its Madonna.
Courtesy Historical de la Grande Guerre.

at Ieper (Ypres) and the shell-damaged cathedral at Rheims. Less common, at least in European collections, are examples of American shell case Trench Art, such as the 75mm French shell, also at the Historial, which is embossed with the American Eagle and has several inscriptions 'A.E.F', 'James', 'John and Mattie', 'WORLDWAR', and '1914-18-19'. Similarly professional, though much rarer, are shell cases painted with Japanese/Chinese ladies in traditional costume, and others which have been beautifully enamelled and painted with pastoral landscape scenes.

For civilians caught up in the war, whether on the Western Front, the Italian Front, or the Middle East, there was a variety of skills already possessed or quickly acquired. Apart from the skills involved there was also a variety of other, more cultural, factors at work which affected the manufactue of Trench Art. For the Belgians along the banks of the Ijzer (Yser), there was the issue of language, politics, and culture to be addressed. The Belgian copper workers produced some of the most spectacular and sophisticated examples of the genre, but there was another side to the story.

While the ordinary Belgian soldier usually spoke Flemish, the officer class spoke French. This linguistic difference was a sign of the deeper cultural divide between the mainly French south and the pre-

Fig. 3.23: French 75mm artillery shell case decorated with the American Eagle and the letters AEF.

Fig. 3.24: Enamelled artillery shell case. Blue-on-white painting depicts a snowy landscape and shattered house, with the inscription 'Yser 1914-1918', and signed 'H.J.'
Courtesy Historical de la Grande Guerre

dominantly Flemish north. The Ijzer (Yser) area, especially around the city of Diksmuide, was then, and remains today, a focus of Flemish nationalism. This political tension found artistic expression in Trench Art. One of the recurring motifs engraved or embossed onto the shell case vases made by these soldiers was a rampant Flanders Lion – an artistic symbol of the political aspirations of the Flemish people – and one which today can be seen everywhere in Flanders. The lion was

Fig. 3.25: Gabriel Versavel, in June 2000. He watched and helped his two uncles make Trench Art in 1916 and 1917.

Fig. 3.26: The Versavel Windmill.
Author copyright with acknowledgement to the Versavel Archive

Fig. 3.27: The Versavel Cannon.
Author copyright with acknowledgement to the Versavel Archive

often accompanied by inscriptions in Flemish. Today, these most exquisite of all decorated Trench Art shell cases fetch the highest prices in Belgium – a symbol of the war and of the continuing struggle between these two peoples in a united Europe.

Occasionally, there is a body of work which stands out, by virtue of the inventive genius of its civilian makers, and because it was made only during the war years. Jules and Camiel Versavel were brothers from the town of Passchendaele who, along with

Fig. 3.28: One of several elaborate crucifixes made by the Versavel brothers. Mounted on a 1915 German shell 126mm shell case base with lion's claw feet and a cross of brass and copper. The figures are commercially made.

Author copyright with acknowledgement to the Versavel Archive

the rest of the family, evacuated the town in 1916 for a safer area behind the Allied lines near Poperinge a few miles outside Ieper (Ypres). Here, between 1916 and 1917, they created some extraordinary works of metal Trench Art – all the more striking as neither was a trained metalsmith, neither had made such objects before, and neither was ever to make them again after the war.

The family's private collection is a treasure house of Trench Art made more valuable by the fact that ninety-eight year old Gabriel Versavel, the nephew of Jules and Camiel, is still alive and remarkably fit and sharp (in June 2000). He vividly remembers collecting up raw materials for his uncles to make their masterpieces. In this collection, some of which is illustrated here, is an astonishing windmill, made in commemoration of Passchendaele's landmark windmill destroyed in the war. The body is a German artillery shell manufactured in Magdeburg in February 1916, with a circular 'walkway' composed of rifle bullets in sequences of three – French, Belgian and British. Equally impressive is an elaborate cannon made from a 1916 British 6-pounder shell and mounted on drive-band wheels. There are also a series of crosses made from scrap metal and copper drive-bands, several with commercially made Christ figures attached.

Fig. 3.29: The Versavel toolkit.

In the Streeksmuseum in the nearby town of Zonnebeke is a small collection of Trench Art in a glass-fronted display case. Interesting and representative as it is, what makes it especially valuable is a set of Trench Art making tools. These were made by the Versavel brothers themselves to fashion their art, and were donated by the family during the 1970s. Today, the case of the Versavel family is unique, with the memories of Gabriel breathing life and poignancy into the objects and implements made in front of his eyes by two long-dead uncles in the dark years of 1916-1917.

In one of the other main theatres of war, the Middle East, there was a different form of expression in decorated shell cases. Large numbers of British, Australian and New Zealand troops operated in the region from Greece and Turkey to Egypt and Palestine. This area was home to long established Arab metalworking traditions, often family based, with goods for sale in local souks or bazaars. While many soldiers doubtless made shell case Trench Art in the ways described above, they also appear to have taken advantage of the available local skills. Arab craftsmen made often exquisitely decorated shell cases for the large numbers of Allied soldiers passing through the region. There were two main kinds of this art. First, there were examples which simply transferred

Fig. 3.30: 1915 German 75mm artillery shell case, decorated in Arab style with Islamic calligraphy in silver and copper.

motifs of sphinxes, pyramids and seated pharaohs which had been used to decorate pre-war souvenir art for Europeans. Second, was the non-pictorial style which followed more traditional themes and designs from Islamic calligraphy. The example shown here was

Fig. 3.31: Tabacco or tea container made from two 4.5 inch howitzer shell cases decorated with Islamic calligraphy.

Fig. 3.32: Dinner gong made from a 75mm shell case decorated with the Sphinx, and with the words 'Egypt' and 'Lincolnshire' and mounted on a wooden frame engraved with the year '1919'.

made from the bases of two 4.5 inch Howitzer shells and probably served to hold tobacco or tea. While some of these were probably made 'on spec', others would have been commissioned, and yet others may have been half made by local craftsmen and perhaps finished off by a soldier inscribing his own name or unit details.

An interesting minority of Trench Art shell case pieces were made for, or adapted to, overtly religious purposes, especially by French soldiers, whose Catholicism integrated icons into religious devotion more readily than their Protestant comrades. The terrible losses of manpower in the French army lead to sporadic outbreaks of what amounted almost to idolatry in the trenches where religious activities focused on silver-plated shell cases adorned with soldered-on crosses.

Perhaps one of the most ironic kinds of artillery shell Trench Art were those made into dinner-gongs. Commercially made dinner-gongs had long been a common feature of Victorian and Edwardian middle class life in Britain. Perhaps inspired by these pre-war domestic examples, and possibly also by earlier Trench Art examples from the Boer War, Great War soldiers took to suspending single shell cases in their trenches to be struck as an alarm, warning of a gas attack. In this way, the hitherto civilized sounds of homely mealtimes were transformed, initiating a desperate scramble to don gas masks and avoid excruciatingly painful debilitation, blindness or death. After the war, the process was reversed. Shell cases, decorated and plain, were suspended from small wooden frames as souvenir dinner-gongs. Only now their sounding announced lunch or dinner rather than a deadly threat. The feelings of many returning soldiers on hearing these sounds can only be imagined.

Fig. 3.33: Masonic shell-clock with bullet legs, made from a First World War brass shell, and dedicated to the 'Michigan Lodge No.50, Jackson, Mich.' It is painted with an American shield, French and American flags, and decorated with Masonic designs. The designs, along with the numbers and letters, have been individually cut into the metal.
Courtesy of Phoenix Masonry Inc

Chapter 4

A WORLD OF METALS

The same makers of Trench Art shell cases also made a variety of other metal items. While the ordinary soldier and civilian made what they could from available scrap, the more sophisticated pieces were made by those either with metalworking experience, or, as in the case of the Versavel brothers, a talent for crafting items with specialist tools in locations that provided a degree of safety.

There was, as the chapter on classification has shown, a large number of different kinds of objects made, from writing sets, pens and pencils, cigarette lighters, serviette rings, clocks, jewellery, and a host of miniatures, from tanks to ships and aeroplanes. In addition there was a seemingly universal penchant among servicemen for personalizing their own equipment and the commercially made items which they bought or acquired. These items, when considered together, seem to make up a world of metal objects which are distinguished by their functionality and portability rather than size and ornamentality, though as expected, there are exceptions to this rule of thumb.

Many items, like those of the Chinese labour corps already mentioned, were made on an opportunistic basis for sale or barter. Indicative of this is an extraordinary cache of complete and half-finished letter-openers and bullets decorated with badges from various regiments in the Liddle Collection at Leeds University. Made by the Royal Engineers, they were stored inside two polished and lidded 4.5 inch Howitzer shell case bases. Almost certainly they would have been made in a permanent workshop area or perhaps one of the mobile workshops that the Royal Engineers used.

Even more remarkable, are the beautifully crafted Trench Art objects made by Sapper Stanley K. Pearl of the Australian 5th Field Company Engineers kept now in the Australian War Memorial in Canberra. These include a hat-pin stand in the form of a daisy and made from parts of army bicycles, a German water bottle, a 77mm shell case and an 18-pounder nose-cap; a rose bowl decorated with German buttons removed from dead enemy soldiers; and a scoop made from a Hales rifle-grenade, a 77mm shell case and a Royal Engineers badge taken

Fig. 4.1: Sapper Pearl's clock.
Courtesy Australian War Memorial

from a sapper wounded by Baron von Richthofen's 'flying circus'. What makes these pieces so unusual is that, as is evident, Sapper Pearl kept detailed notes on each piece, documenting where and when he gathered the constituent parts and what, if any, associations they had for him. These documents provide a unique glimpse of the wealth of information and associated memories which must have been a feature of countless examples of Trench Art but which are now largely lost. An illustration of how a soldier's physical and mental worlds could be embodied in a single object are strikingly apparent in Pearl's notes on his making of a Trench Art clock. It was, he says,

'Made at Ypres in March 1918. The case was made from two 4.5-inch shell-cases picked up on Christmas Day 1917 at the Australian batteries at Le Bizet. The foot support is a clip of an 18-pounder shell. The arms are detonator wells of rifle-grenades and nose-caps. The hands are from a gun-cotton case, while the alarm cover is an American-made 18-pounder nose-cap with a "whizz-bang" driving-band. The Rising Sun is the badge of a mate killed at Noreuil, while a button from the maker's greatcoat and a German bullet surmount the whole.'

Writing Equipment

Clocks were a popular kind of Trench Art for those who could make them. More easily made, and thus more common, were letter-openers of which many different kinds have survived. The most common is that with a bullet as a handle and a crescent blade made from scrap brass or the reworked copper of a drive-band. More unusual are those cast from a single piece of shrapnel where the handle is left unworked and the blade is honed straight. Although these items were made probably in their tens of thousands, sometimes an example comes to light with a story which seems to nail it into history. Such is the case of the account preserved in the London Irish Rifles Regimental Museum of the making of a bullet letter-opener.

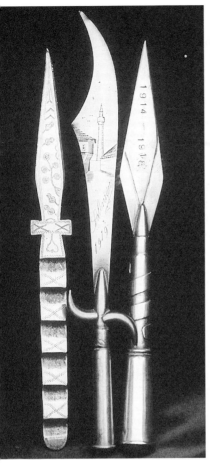

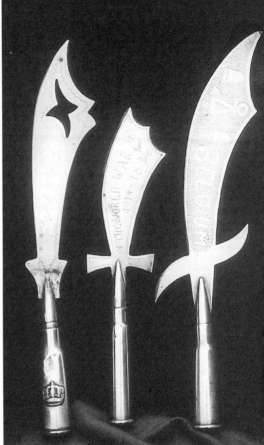

Fig. 4.2: Three kinds of letter openers:
left to right – a. made from copper
drive-band; b. made from .303 bullet
and 'Saloniqe 1919' on brass blade; and
c. elaborate composite copper-brass
blade with two bullets and with '1914-
1918' on blade.

Fig. 4.3: Three crescent-blade letter
openers: left to right, made from Belgian
bullet with 'Reims' engraved on blade;
made from .303 bullet with 'The World
War 1914-18' on blade; and Belgian
bullet with 'ASP' and 'Belgium' on the
blade.

Fig. 4.4: French soldier making a letter
opener from a copper drive-band.

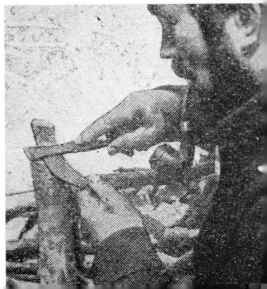

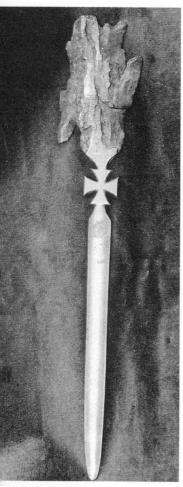

Fig. 4.5: German letter opener cast from a single piece of shrapnel.
Author copyright with acknowledgement to Philipe Oosterlinck

In November 1915, the 1st Battalion, London Irish Rifles was on the Western Front, in the area north of Arras. They had spent the evening of the 14th sampling the restaurants and bars of Lillers, and by 8.30 a.m. the following day were marching along the road in bright sunshine towards Raimbert where they were to undertake several weeks of training. That night the weather broke and on the morning of the 16th the ground was covered in snow. At some time during the march, or perhaps upon arrival at Raimbert, one enterprising soldier had made a letter-opener from several rifle cartridges and inscribed it '15th November, 1915'.

Even more insightful, though in a different way, is the account left by Sapper Pearl of his fashioning of several letter-openers – one of which again provides a glimpse of a long lost soldier's war.

'The blade is from a slice of an 18-pounder shell-case found near the "China Wall" at Ypres in November 1916. The handle is a French cartridge-case and spent German bullet – the latter fired at a party of sappers on the Menin road. The copper disc is another piece of the Gotha's feed pipe with French and German bullets (split). The French button was souvenired from a poilu in Poperinge.'

Letter-openers, or paper knives as they are also called, had a clear function in the Great War, where letter writing was prevalent. They also possessed a deeply ironic aspect by virtue of the fact that they were made of the weapons that caused the most devastation to the human body. In a symbolic sense, they connected a soldier's extraordinary trench experiences with 'normal' life at home – itself a precarious relationship carried on in precious fragments of time represented by the writing and reading of letters. How many tender and poignant missives were opened with an implement that had killed or maimed another human being ?

Probably as common as the instruments which opened letters were those used to write them. Ever since bullets had been made they were probably also used to make pencils and pens. The author has seen one made from a British bullet, engraved with 'Omdurman' on one side, and 'Remember Gordon' on the other, and presumably dating to the battle of Omdurman in 1898. Others were made during the Boer War of 1899-1902. This tradition probably influenced the soldiers of the Great War but there is also the unusual appearance of bullet-pencils being included in the gift set given to all non-smoking soldiers (smokers received a more flammable gift) by the Princess Mary's Gift Fund in 1914, along with a khaki writing case, paper, envelopes, a Christmas card and a photograph of the Princess. Some examples were two-in-one writing implements, whereby two bullet cartridges were welded together, and of the two removable bullets, one had been made into a pencil, the other a pen nib.

Often, bullet pens/pencils and letter-openers were made singly for sale or barter – commonplace items of everyday life for the soldier. However, sometimes they were part of a more elaborate 'writing set'. Some of these were basic indeed – made from scrap metal cut and filed to shape in the trenches, while others were more elaborate, probably made by Royal Engineers or professional

Fig. 4.6: Ambiguous letter-opener/dagger. Made from a flechette (anti-personnel spike dropped from aeroplanes), Belgian bullet handle, and British .303 bullet cartridge as sheath.

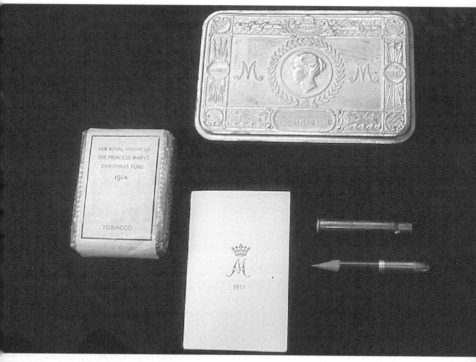

Fig. 4.7: Princess Mary's Gift Fund set 1914, including a bullet-pencil.

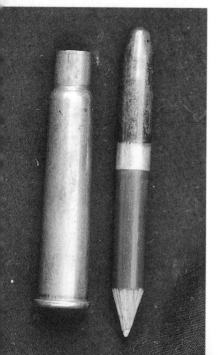

metalsmiths. The second example shown here almost certainly was made by Belgian soldier-metalsmiths on the Ijzer (Yser) front. These examples were made from scrap brass, sometimes decorated with a horseshoe and/or copper drive-bands, and had bent bullets (usually French) welded on to support a letter-opener and pen/pencil. Many had a fuze cap whose top had been removed then hinged in order to create an inkwell.

If we imagine a serviceman sitting down to write a letter with all these implements made from the transformed detritus of war we might easily also

Fig. 4.8: Bullet-pencil from Princess Mary's Gift set 1914.

Fig. 4.9: Bullet pen-pencil made from two cartridges welded end to end.

Fig. 4.10: Basic writing set made from scrap brass, with a fuze-cap inkwell, and surmounted by a copper drive-band shaped as a horseshoe.

imagine a photograph of a loved one in front of him as he wrote to his mother, wife or sweetheart. It comes as no surprise to learn that photograph frames also were made from a variety of scrap metals sometimes adorned with bullet cartridges. In fact many were also made from wood, and in one unusual example in the Imperial War Museum, of an army issue biscuit.

By chance, we have a remarkable first-hand account of the making of a Trench Art photograph frame. As with the notes kept by Sapper Pearl, the details of this example also reveal how a single object can contain memories of the war and its often striking personal details.

Lance Corporal Reginald Bunn was born in 1894, and served as a blacksmith in the British army from 24 April 1917 until 25 January

1919, in the 342 RCCRE attd Road Workshops Fifth Army. Bunn was the son of the village blacksmith at North Burlingham, Norwich, and worked there with his father in the early years of the war. He was recruited when he was twenty-three. His commanding officer was later to comment that Bunn was a dutiful and highly skilled blacksmith who turned out excellent work.

On at least one occasion, this work included a piece of Trench Art in the form of a photograph frame. In his own words, which have the spontaneity of first-hand witness, he says:

'I made it myself under circumstances over which I had no control, hence the crude workmanship. After the Armistice in 1918 we came back to a shell-damaged margarine factory at a place called Fivees [Fives] outside the big city of Lille, which had been captured by us earlier. This factory had a workshop and here I made the enclosed. The copper plate I cut from the case which had contained Ammonal. A very high explosive sent for tunnelling and other purposes. The bullets at the corners were rifle bullets used by the French Infantry. The shoes I made from the copper driving band of a German high velocity shell (the calibre of the gun I forget). This came (I picked it up whilst still hot) from the famous Vimy Ridge, captured later by the Canadians. (I was at Vimy Ridge in

Fig. 4.11: Elaborate writing set, probably made from Belgian soldier-metalsmiths. The horese-shoe shaped copper drive-band says 'Yser', beneath is the Flanders Lion motif, a bullet and a copper-bladed letter-opener is supported on bullets, and the fuze-cap inkwell is engraved 'Souvenir'.

Fig. 4.12: Lance Corporal Reginald Bunn.
Courtesy Christopher Basey

Fig. 4.13: Trench Art photograph frame made by Lance Corporal Reginald Bunn.
Courtesy Christopher Basey

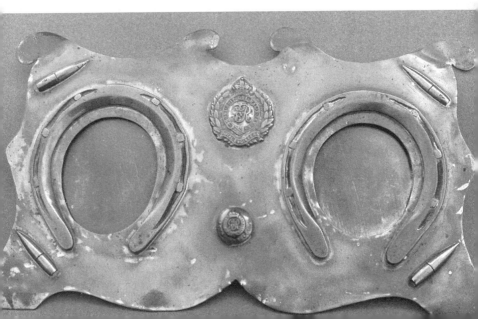

April 1917). The horse shoe nails I made from our own cartridge case. The pieces of glass I think I can remember getting these from a totally wrecked billiard saloon in Bethune.

Smoking Equipment

The vast majority of Great War soldiers were smokers. For every two servicemen who received the non-smokers variety of Princess Mary's 1914 gift set, fifty-six received the smoker's version. This represented a huge potential market for Trench Art oriented to the tobacco addict and consequently smoking related items are some of the most frequently encountered.

Perhaps the most ubiquitous of these is the matchbox cover, usually made of brass but sometimes also in steel and occasionally iron. Usually these were simple sheets of scrap cut into shape and folded over to leave open sides into which the matchbox could be slid. Simple designs and inscriptions could easily be engraved by the ordinary soldier almost anywhere, and these were often supplemented by the soldering on of cap badges, tunic buttons and sectioned bullets. As mentioned previously, some of these items were

Fig. 4.14: British 4.5 inch howitzer shell base surmounted by a French Dragoon and used to store tobacco. 'Poperinghe' is etched around the base.

made by civilians for the soldiers on both sides, and the typically German inscription 'Gott Mit Uns' is not a reliable indicator that the piece was made by German soldiers. Matchbox covers without a date or giveaway motif are notoriously difficult to assign to a specific category, and identical items were made by active servicemen (in dugouts and behind the lines) and civilians during the war, by civilians

Fig. 4.14: Decorated soldier's pipe made from a bullet cartridge stem and aluminium bowl, engraved 'Iser'.

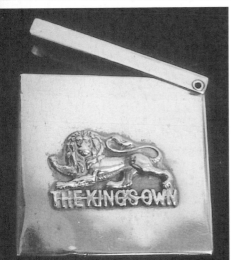

Fig. 4.16: Cigarette case made from scrap brass and decorated with crest of The King's Own Royal Regiment (Lancaster).

Fig. 4.17: Four matchbox covers made from copper and brass.

Fig. 4.19: Two brass matchbox covers, one with 'Gott mit uns', the other with a German pickelhaube helmet.

Fig. 4.18: Composite matchbox-ashtray made from a bullet cartridge and mounted on a brass artillery shell base, engraved 'Souvenir De L'Yser 1913.'

Fig. 4.20: Matchbox cover made by a soldier possibly in the trenches. Its design suggests that it was made by a soldier of the Lancashire Fusiliers whose badge is next to it.
Author copyright and acknowledgement to Philipe Oosterlinck.

Fig. 4.21: Reverse side of this matchbox cover shows the name of the maker 'Tom Hodgson'.
Author copyright and acknowledgement to Philipe Oosterlinck.

after the war, and by various individuals in prisoner of war and civilian internment camps.

One example which still retains its military and historical associations is that currently on display at the London Irish Rifles Regimental Museum. On 4 May, 1918, the 2nd battalion, London Irish Rifles, was engaged in operations east of the River Jordan in Palestine, when it were attacked by four enemy planes. One, a German 'Albatros', was shot down near a spot called Gray's Hill, and was totally destroyed and the pilot killed. Along with a map showing exactly where this event took place, the Regimental War Diary for 1918 relates that, 'An aluminium Match-box cover was made from a piece of this crashed aeroplane.' The piece itself is inscribed (in fact, faintly scratched) with 'German Plane No. 3188. Brought Down In Palestine IV May 1918. By L.REH'.

One particular kind of matchbox cover was made during the inter-war years, and has recently enjoyed a curious revival. During the 1920s, when large numbers of pilgrims began visiting the Ieper (Ypres) region, local industry had become sufficiently re-established to start making brass matchbox covers (and ashtrays) decorated with photogravure images of local landmarks such as the Hill 60 Memorial, the rebuilt Cloth Hall at Ieper (Ypres), and the Menin Gate – all of which date to this period. In the 1970s, reproductions of these were

Fig. 4.22: Pair of 1970s photogravure matchbox covers showing the Menin Gate and the Cloth Hall at Ieper (Ypres).

commercially made from thin industrial metals and can still be found on sale today, having themselves become collectable imitations of inter-war Trench Art.

Cigarette lighters also were popular and came in a seemingly endless variety of shapes and forms. A favourite was some variation of the bullet-lighter, where one or several bullet cartridges were filled with a wick and petrol, with a simple flint-and-wheel mechanism attached. Sometimes these were very basic, other times more elaborate, with badges and buttons soldered onto the cartridge. Occasionally a small lighter mechanism was fixed onto a hinge which slid into a small metal 'book', the surface of which could then be engraved with the owners initials. Other examples could be similarly 'disguised' as miniature aeroplanes, tanks or as officers peaked caps.

A typically French design was the disc-shaped lighter which has what appears to be commercially made circular plaques welded onto each side. These plaques portray a profile of a large-nosed soldier's head, wearing a soft cap – in fact a caricature of the German General Crown Prince Wilhelm. Sometimes, as with the one shown here, small insciptions were added – in this case one side says 'Mon Reve' (My Dream), with 'Paris' lightly scratched onto the soldier's collar, while the other side is inscribed with 'L'eau De La Marne Est Amère' (The Water of the Marne is Bitter) and this time 'Verdun' appears on the collar. On the Paris side the Crown Prince's mouth is upturned in a smile, while on the Verdun side, the mouth is downturned and tears fall from the eye. Such lighters seem to embody not just the frustrated attempts of the German High Command to capture Verdun and leave

Fig. 4.25: Hungarian ash-tray lighter made from the base of a 1914 100mm artillery shell and decorated in art nouveau style.

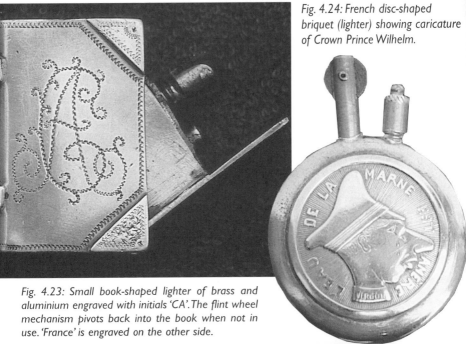

Fig. 4.24: French disc-shaped briquet (lighter) showing caricature of Crown Prince Wilhelm.

Fig. 4.23: Small book-shaped lighter of brass and aluminium engraved with initials 'CA'. The flint wheel mechanism pivots back into the book when not in use. 'France' is engraved on the other side.

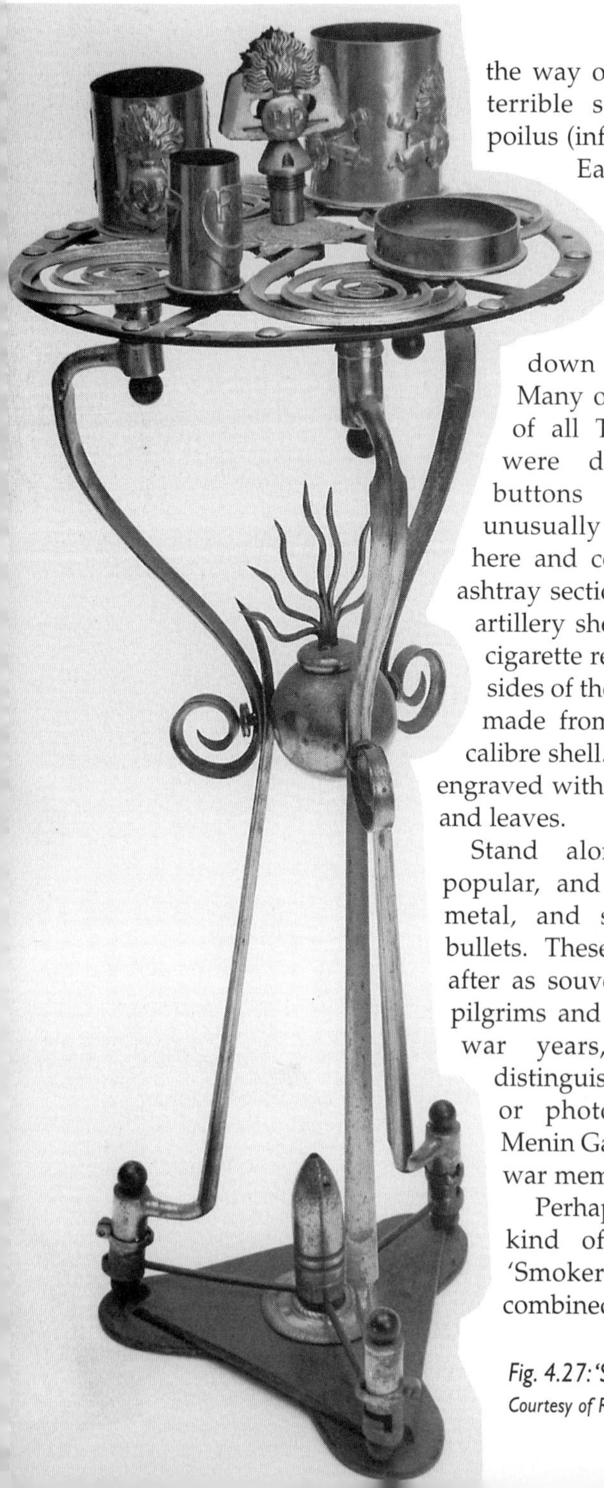

the way open to Paris, but also the terrible sufferings of the French poilus (infantry-men) in the 'Hell on Earth' that Verdun had become.

Sometimes cigarette lighters were combined with ashtrays which were made from the cut down base of artillery shells. Many of these are the most basic of all Trench Art, though some were decorated with badges, buttons and inscriptions. An unusually fine example is shown here and comes from Hungary. The ashtray section is the base of a 100mm artillery shell, dated 1914, with three cigarette rests 'turned over' from the sides of the shell, and the lighter part made from an unidentified smaller calibre shell. Both parts are beautifully engraved with art nouveau style flowers and leaves.

Stand alone ashtrays too were popular, and were made from scrap metal, and sometimes fringed with bullets. These were especially sought after as souvenirs made for battlefield pilgrims and visitors during the inter-war years, and can be easily distinguished by a memorial plaque or photogravure image of the Menin Gate (1927) or a similar post-war memorial.

Perhaps the most unusual of this kind of item is the so-called 'Smokers Companion', which combined all of the above features

Fig. 4.27: 'Smokers Companion'.
Courtesy of Roy Butler, Wallis and Wallis

Fig. 4.28: Aluminium identity tag for D H Preston, dated 5. 5. 16, inscribed Salonika.

Fig. 4.26: Post-war souvenir ashtray of brass decorated with bullets.

into one elaborate contraption made of all kinds of war *matériel* such as the one illustrated here and sold at auction in 1999. Referred to by yet another term as a 'Trophy of Arms', it stands just under three feet tall, is mounted on six triangular socket bayonets with a flaming grenade at the intersection. The 'table' is of four spiral épée blades and is surmounted by four small but decorated Trench Art shell cases and a cartridge clip matchbox holder. All these items have badges attached. This elaborate kind of Trench Art was apparently especially popular with French soldiers.

Such is the number and diversity of these smokers' objects that one sometimes loses sight of the irony of soldiers living in appalling conditions bothering to use an ashtray in the filth and destruction which surrounded them, both at the front and in rear areas.

Jewellery, Miniatures, and Miscellanea

One of the easiest to make and most popular kinds of Trench Art

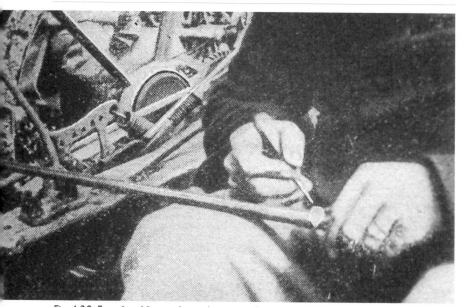

Fig. 4.29: French soldier making aluminium finger ring.

Fig. 4.30: Assortment of aluminium finger rings with copper inlay.

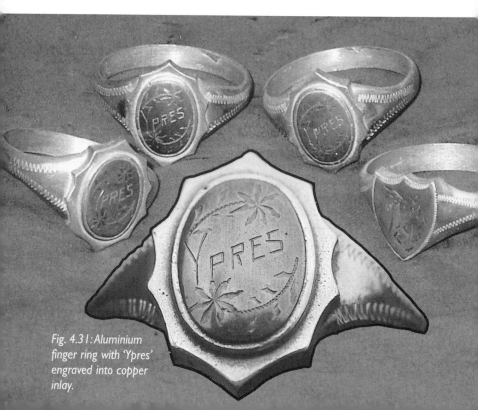

Fig. 4.31: Aluminium finger ring with 'Ypres' engraved into copper inlay.

Fig. 4.32: Commercially made German bracelet made of Belgian one Cent coins and minature Iron Crosses with dates '1914', 1915', '1916'.

Fig. 4.34: Trench Art jewellery made from scrap aluminium. Bought by Staff Nurse M G Trembath, it commemorates the Regatta of 1918 at Amarna, Mesopotamia.
Author copyright and acknowledgement to the Imperial War Museum

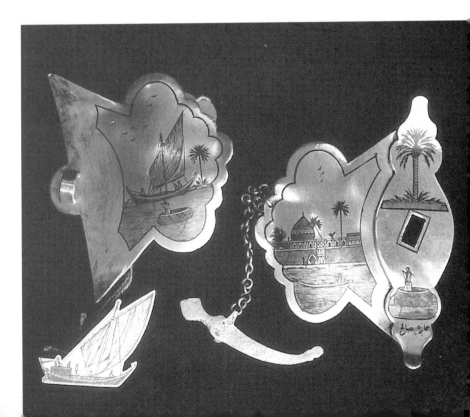

Kriegs- Erinnerungs-
Siegelringe

Ring Nr. 1039.

Echt 800 Silber

Jeder Ring ist gesetzlich gestempelt.
Platte gehämmert, mit Kreuz in echt Emai
mit echt 800 Silber ausgelegt

Reklamepreis M. 1,80

sowie 20 Pfg. für Porto und Verpackung,
wenn Sie uns diesen Betrag per Postan-
weisung oder in Papiergeld bzw. Brief-
marken einsenden. Nachnahmen ins Feld
sind nicht zulässig. Als Ringgrösse genügt
ein Papierstreifen. Verlangen Sie sofor
gratis und franko unseren neuen Katalog
über Kriegs-Andenken nebst Ringmass.

Sims & Mayer,
Berlin E., Oranienstrasse 117/118.

Fig. 4.33: Contemporary German advertisement for commercially made finger rings.

Fig. 4.35: Trench Art owl made from cartridge bases and scrap brass.

Fig. 4.36: Fuze cap mounted by three bullets.

Fig. 4.37: German cast iron (?) 'jar', sometimes described as an officer's drinking cup, but also a traditional form used throughout Europe as a mortar for mixing medicines, and pounding coffee beans, and walnuts.

was jewellery – though some might quibble at this description. Many soldiers made wristbands from the readily available copper drive-bands of shells, sometimes in their raw state, and other times inscribed. Earrings, finger rings, and personalized identity tags, were all made in large quantities, sometimes for the soldiers themselves, and equally often as souvenirs for relatives, wives, and sweethearts back home.

While Allied troops favoured Trench Art jewellery, German soldiers seemed to prefer commercially made items, bracelets made of coins and miniature Iron Crosses, and rings stamped with the Iron Cross and/or Weltkrieg (World War). Wartime German newspapers and periodicals are full of advertisements for all these kinds of objects – none of which qualify as Trench Art as we have defined it. Sometimes, the common and the rare were combined into a commercially elaborated kind of Trench Art – such as wrist-bands made of copper drive-bands picked up on the battlefield and then gold- or silver-plated. These various kinds of objects are referred to by several different names – 'Mourning Jewellery' (especially in Europe) and 'Sweetheart Jewellery' (mainly in Britain) being the most common. One example shows how broad this kind of Trench Art can be – it is a brooch made from a Zeppelin bomb which had been found at Spurn Point in England. Almost certainly a fine and important distinction could be made between Mourning Jewellery and Sweetheart Jewellery, though this is beyond the scope of this present book.

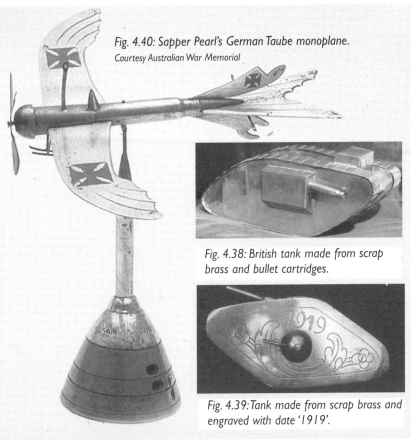

Fig. 4.40: Sapper Pearl's German Taube monoplane.
Courtesy Australian War Memorial

Fig. 4.38: British tank made from scrap brass and bullet cartridges.

Fig. 4.39: Tank made from scrap brass and engraved with date '1919'.

Fig. 4.41: Large Trench Art biplane, with wooden propellers and a fuselage of a French 75mm shell case. It is 56 centimetres long and maximum wingspan is 59 centimetres.
Courtesy Historial de la Grande Guerre

Fig. 4.42: Decorative talismanic bullet /button-hook, engraved for 'Frank'.

Despite the obvious functional nature of these (and numerous other) objects, a host of more idiosyncratic items were also made. Some of these are either ambiguous or obviously non-functional. An example of the former is an officer's 'swagger stick', artfully made from bullets and currently held in the Imperial War Museum, with another splendid example in the 'Flanders Fields Museum' in Ieper, Belgium. As for purely ornamental pieces, miniatures of real life war machines were commonly made. These include aircraft (monoplanes, biplanes and triplanes) painstakingly made from bullet cartridge cases and miscellaneous metal scrap, various sizes of tanks from a few inches long to several feet, and different shapes and sizes of battleships. Tanks and ships were also, and possibly more frequently, made in wood.

Amongst some of the most beautifully made miniature aeroplanes are those which represent the German Taube monoplane with its characteristic feather-like swept-back wings. Sapper Pearl relates, in typical detail, how he made one on the Somme in January 1917. The fuselage is of French and German bullet cartridges, the wings and tail were cut from a German water bottle found at Flers, and the propeller is a piece of the lining of a cordite charge box from a 6 inch Howitzer battery found near Waterlot Farm. While many of these miniature aeroplanes are indeed small, some, like the magnificent biplane in the storeoom of the Historial de la Grande Guerre are huge by comparison, with the fuselage made not from a bullet cartridge but an artillery shell case.

Many of these small and portable objects were highly personalized, sometimes engraved with a man's name, and occasionally rank, regiment and geographical location. While some soldiers undoubtedly made these themselves, the majority were probably 'mass produced', with soldiers paying to have their name inscribed on the artefact or scratching their name onto a professionally made item.

A more poignant example of 'naming' a portable piece of Trench Art is the talismanic bullet, described in context in chapter six. These could be simple defused bullet cartridges with a name scratched into the

Fig. 4.43: Holy water dispenser made from aluminium and adorned with commercially made angels figures.
Author copyright with acknowledgement to the Versavel Archive

metal, or elaborately decorated examples which were also functional as with the example shown here which opens to reveal a metal button-hook.

For the more religious soldier – especially, but not only, the Catholic French poilu – the propensity of Christianity to integrate icons into religious devotions affected the forms and uses of certain kinds of metal Trench Art made by servicemen. Quite common were the holy water dispensers strategically located in a trench so that every soldier could be blessed when going into the line. Although any receptacle could be used for this purpose, inverted aluminium or brass shell nose cones were a favourite device, often attached to a sometimes shaped scrap of brass. More spectacular were the wartime versions of bullet-crucifixes, made by servicemen and civilians and carried by soldiers into battle. More elaborate versions of these crucifixes were made as souvenirs after the war.

Another example of small scale religiously inspired Trench Art is held at the National Maritime Museum at Greenwich, and which has rare accompanying documentation. This is a German bullet and cartridge case fashioned into a cross by a French poilu and subsequently acquired and used by a chaplain of The Royal Naval Division on the Western Front. When in the field, he placed it on a gun wheel where it served as an altar for religious services. As with the silver-plated artillery shells adorned with a cross, the Great War produced a strange kind of religious activity where the objects which caused so much devastation to the human body and landscape were also used to make objects of religious devotion.

The Victoria Cross

One of the most remarkable examples of Trench Art is also one of the least expected. Its story brings together conflict, bravery, metal, and a unique set of historical resonances, even though it is not restricted to the Great War.

Of all the world's medals given for bravery in battle only one can be classed as Trench Art – and that is the most famous. The Victoria Cross was instituted in 1856 and first awarded, retrospectively, for valour, in the Crimean War 1854-1855. What makes the Victoria Cross Trench Art are the unique circumstances surrounding its origins. During the Crimean War, China gave Russia bronze cannon to fight the British and these were captured by the British at the battle of Sebastopol. The

Fig. 4.44: Russian bronze cannon at Sebastopol in the Redan Redoubt, where they had been abandoned by the Russian gunners on the night of 8th September, 1855.

breeches of these guns were melted down into ingots of bronze kept now by the Ministry of Defence. When a VC is awarded, a rough cast of the Cross is made and hand finished by Hancocks Jewellers of London. The one remaining ingot is probably sufficient to make a further eighty Crosses.

All other official medals are made from

Fig. 4.44a: Victoria Cross. Enough metal remains for a further eighty medals.

commercial metals and therefore the material has no story to tell in and of itself. Such medals commemorate one event – the individual act of bravery for which they are awarded. The Victoria Cross, however, as metal recycled and reworked from the weapons of a nineteenth century war, qualifies as a unique kind of Trench Art whose raw material is a physical link to the past, and recalls over 150 years of previous acts of valour as well as the one for which it is individually awarded. The metal itself, before it is even shaped into a Cross, is valued and guarded as a repository of historical, military, and wider cultural significance.

Fig. 4.45: Trench Art battlefield memorial to French General Estienne, creator of the French Armoured Forces, near the Moulin de Laffaux north of Soissons. It commemorates a tank battle 5th and 6th May 1917 and has a recycled Renault tank wheel and aluminium sheets forming a cross motif.

Chapter 5

WOOD, TEXTILE AND BONE

Metal Trench Art has received the majority of interest from collectors due to its easily identifiable connections to the Great War. Nevertheless there are many other three dimensional objects which can also be considered. These include objects carved in wood, bone and chalk, as well as certain kinds of graffiti, and a vast amount of textile work, such as embroidered and/or painted cloth, and items of beadwork (the last two often appearing on the same piece). These items were by and large easier to fashion than metal objects, and tended to be produced more by the common soldier with makeshift tools in the trenches than those with access to the more specialized metalworking equipment. The range of such objects is vast, though as a general rule their nature meant that they belonged more to the war years than the inter-war period. Nevertheless, there are important distinctions to be made, not least when it comes to assessing the role of some items as therapy for the war-maimed. All can be considered Trench Art as we have defined it, and all reveal different aspects of their maker's war experience.

Fig. 5.1:Wooden photograph frame in the shape of a soldier playing a bugle. It outlines the words 'He volunteered when duty called'.

Woodwork

As our classification reveals, wooden Trench Art comes in a seemingly infinite variety of shapes and forms and, due to the ease with which the raw material could be obtained and worked, is probably the oldest kind of Trench Art in the

Fig. 5.3: Carved wooden box from the Eastern Front dated 1917.

Fig. 5.4: Clock made from the centre boss of a Sopwith Camel's wooden propeller.

Fig. 5.2: Wooden tobacco jar with aluminium inlays. The inscription around the lid says 'TABAC. 1914. MUNSTER. 1915'.
Courtesy Historical de la Grande Guerre

world. During the Great War, soldiers of all sides carved or whittled wood in the safer areas behind the lines, in trenches, dugouts, and even in shell craters when they found themselves forced to take cover on open ground. More than any other kind of Trench Art, wooden objects have the aura of immediacy, of being made in view of the enemy, and of embodying the variable artistic abilities of their makers.

In museums which have Trench Art there are a seemingly endless variety of wooden objects – sometimes humble carvings, other times sophisticated masterpieces. A common type is the carved wooden box, used either for cigarettes, tobacco, matches or perhaps all of these. The rustic nature of these items suggests they were made by ordinary soldiers as, particularly on the Western Front, officers usually had access to more expensive commercially made items sent from home or bought while on leave. The example shown here is from the Eastern Front, a simple but evocative item dated 1917. Another example is made from polished brown wood in the form of a money-box. Flanking the coin slit are two painted flags – a Union Jack and the French Tricolour. The inscription – 'Groningen 21st June 1915 3rd Year To Jessie Holland' – suggests that it was made by a member of the Royal Naval Division which had escaped Antwerp in 1914, crossed the Dutch border to avoid capture by the Germans, and had been interned there till the war's end. A particularly useful object is a clock made from the wood of a Sopwith Camel propeller.

An especially common wooden item, and one which says a lot about how society has changed during the twentieth century, is the walking stick. While officer's swagger sticks could be made from bullet cartridges, the number of wooden canes far outnumber these. Such objects were a feature of civilian peacetime life before the war and it was only natural that they would be made during wartime as well. Today, apart from countryside walkers and ramblers, and the elderly, they are hardly seen in public use. Many of these walking sticks are

Fig. 5.5: Elaborately carved wooden walking stick, topped with a representation of a beared French soldier.
Courtesy Historical de la Grande Guerre

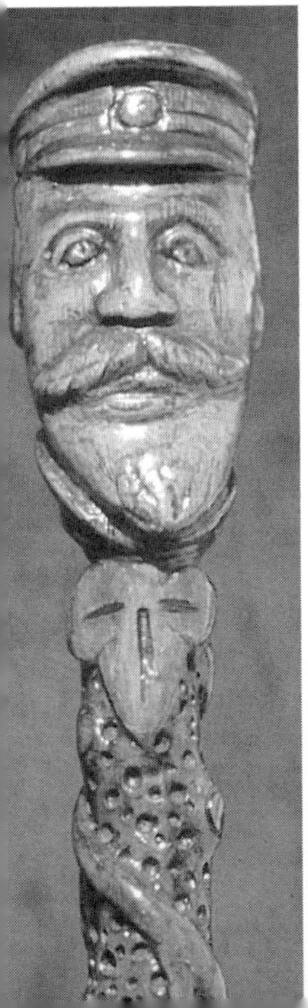

Fig. 5.6: Lacquered walking stick said to represent King George V and acquired from a Canadian officer in Ieper (Ypres).
Author copyright with acknowledgement to the Versavel Archive

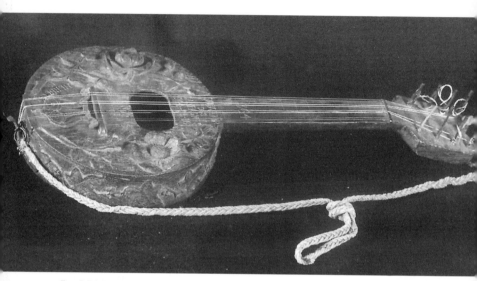

Fig. 5.7: Wooden banjo-like instrument inscibed 'Souvenir Des Campagnes 1914-15-16'
Courtesy Historical de la Grande Guerre

Fig. 5.8: Woodworking shop at Knockaloe Internment Camp, Isle of Man.
Courtesy Manx National Heritage

elaborately carved. The Historial de la Grande Guerre contains beautifully made examples with intricately carved heads – one of which depicts a bearded French soldier beneath which is an inscription, 'Vieux Poilu des Campagnes ou est sa tabacteire 1914-15 1916-17'. In Gabriel Versavel's collection is another example with a head depicting King George V, and which was acquired by one of his uncles in 1917 from a Canadian officer in Ieper (Ypres).

The French poilu had a penchant for making wooden musical instruments, several exquisite examples of which are preserved in the Historial de la Grande Guerre. Perhaps the most interesting is a small banjo-like instrument with all of its eight original wire strings in place. The soundbox is the most elaborately decorated part, its surface covered with intricately carved flowers, including a large rose on one side of the hole and a poppy on the other. There are three inscriptions: 'Souvenir Des Campagnes 1914-15-16', 'Didon Charles', and 'Herbecq E'.

There also exist a large number of miscellaneous wooden items, such as those made from teak said to be from battleships damaged at the battle of Jutland and which were made to raise money for sailors. More unusual is the furniture made in Knockaloe internment camp on the Isle of Man. This was produced to the designs of Charles Rennie Mackintosh under the supervision of Charles Matt who had worked in a London furniture factory before the war. Ironically, these were flatpacked and sent to France in the wake of the German retreat in 1918 – tables, chairs and dressers made by German internees to furnish the temporary housing of their French enemies.

Textiles

Many soldiers and civilians made Trench Art in textiles – either as embroidery (including embroidered postcards), or as painted cloth – usually in the form of handkerchiefs. Many of these were made by local civilians, bought by soldiers, and sent home as souvenirs. On 28 September 1915, Lieutenant E.G. Stewart-Corry wrote home 'I think I'll tell mother that if I come across a

Fig. 5.9: Colour stitched souvenir postcard.

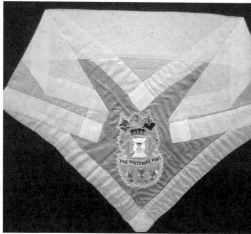

Fig. 5.11: Embroidered souvenir handkerchief, decorated with the crest of the Wiltshire Regiment.

Fig. 5.10: German embroidered textile pouch.
Author copyright acknowledgement to Philipe Oosterlinck

Fig. 5.13: Souvenir embroidery of the crest of the London Irish Rifles.

Fig. 5.15: Embroidered heart-shaped cushion, decorated with coloured beads and bearing the crest of 'Prince Albert's Somerset Light Infantry'.

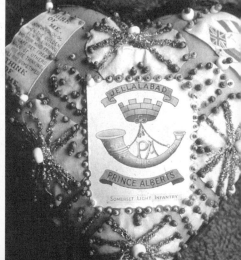

Fig. 5.12: Gilt framed, colour-stitched German memorial textile with photograph of soldier in a shrine-like plaster mount.

handkerchief like the one she mentioned I shall certainly get one.' Especially popular were painted, and sometimes framed, textile images of the Cloth Hall in Ieper (Ypres) in flames, and the leaning Madonna and Child atop the basilica at Albert.

Many men embroidered their regimental crests onto a cloth background as a souvenir for personal use or sale. Many of these have ended up in regimental museums across Britain, such as the beautiful example hanging on the wall of the museum of the London Irish Rifles. Other, almost identical examples had a more poignant aspect as they were made by wounded or maimed soldiers as a way to pass time while convalescing, or specifically as therapy. One of the most popular of these was the heart-shaped decorative cushion sometimes brightly coloured, with a regimental crest embroidered onto it. Often they were decorated with beads, and occasionally also had photographs attached. Empty chocolate boxes were also covered with embroidered designs, such as one which shows a red, white and blue French cockerel surrounded by green leaves and with a dun brown sun and rays above its head. Underneath is preserved the original sticker, 'Confiserie...Bordeaux'.

A more widespread kind of 'soft' Trench Art was the already

Fig. 5.15: Embroidered French chocolate box decorated with a French cockerel grasping a German pickelhaube helmet.
Courtesy Historial de la Grande Guerre

Fig. 5.16: Detail of the head of a snake with small animal gripped in its mouth.

mentioned 'beadwork snake', apparently made by Turkish men both in POW camps in the Middle East and civilian internment camps in Britain. A superb example survives in the Historial de la Grande Guerre. It is 230cm long, with a white underbelly and a light brown dorsal section decorated with white diamond shapes outlined in blue beads, and a head which features a red bead tongue and a four-legged animal (possibly a rat) gripped in its mouth. There are two inscriptions picked out in black beads one says 'Turkish Prisoner', the other '1916'. A host of smaller objects such as ship's anchors, miniature hearts and crucifixes were also made in beadwork.

Bone and Miscellaneous Materials

The most popular kind of Trench Art made from bone were those tens if not hundreds of thousands of items carved from ox bones by active soldiers, the wounded, PoWs, and civilian internees on all sides. As with so many other aspects of Trench Art, a whole book could be written about the differences of style, decoration and significance of

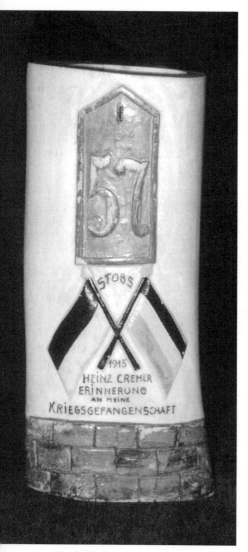

Fig. 5.17: Carved and painted ox bone named for 'Heinz Cremer'.

these items. One piece illustrated here is German, stands 13.5cm in height, depicts a brick wall around the base and a carved and painted set of flags and a regimental shield above. Its inscription reads 'Heinz Cremer Erinnerung An Meine Kriegsgefangenschaft' and is dated to 1915.

Two carved ox bones which illustrate the variability of such objects are in the museum of the King's Own Royal Regiment in Lancaster. One is engraved 'Remembrance 1914-1915 Made in POW Camp Lancaster', and the other 'Lt. E. Smith 5th King's Liverpool Regt. Lancaster Camp 1914-15'. Both could have been made by British soldiers idling away the time or made for them by German prisoners for a price or a long forgotten favour. In the same museum is an unusual safety razor and a letter-opener, also made from bone. In the Historial de la Grande Guerre is a horse scapula painted in oils by a German soldier. One side lists his army comrades, while the other depicts an astonishing battle scene of French Colonial troops (Zouaves) attacking German positions near Soissons on 17 September 1914.

A more unusual, some might say gruesome item, is a small table-top ornament made of wood, and decorated with images of trees and an artillery piece. It has a raised section inscribed 'Honneur Patrie', and is engraved '1914-15' on the left side. Beneath this date is a curious

Fig. 5.18: French soldier flanked by giant chalk carvings.

feature – a small hollowed out section with a broken glass cover surrounded by a roughly incised laurel crown. Inside is a circular piece of bone. The mystery is solved by a piece of paper stuck to the base of the object. When translated it reads, 'Carved by Henri Jarman de Rieucourt for his comrade in arms of 12th RA, Emile Bulot de Selly-Somme wounded and amputated at the arm at Lorette in November 1914.' The bone is a fragment of humerus from Emile's amputated arm.

On a lighter note, were carvings made in or from soft stone, most of which came from northern France. The most famous of these are probably the carved chalk slabs made in and around the Somme region. In Arras there is a small exhibition of these displayed in the chalk tunnels beneath the Hôtel de Ville in the city centre. Interestingly, some of these were made by Maoris serving with the New Zealand forces. Both sides worked in chalk. German soldiers carved plaques with an Iron Cross, dates, and the inevitable 'Gott mit uns', while the British preferred more personal works, such as one shaped into a shield and inscribed 'In memory of Chapel Alley, Verrelles, Septr. 1915.' Another was a memorial to James Crozier carved by a stretcher bearer in the basement of a house in Auchonvillers on the Somme. French soldiers also carved elaborate graffiti and religious images underground, especially along the limestone area of the Chemin des Dames as at the 'Dragon's Cave'. Even more spectacular is the altar at Pierre decorated with a mix of religious and military motifs.

Fig. 5.19: Subterranean chapel carved in the caves at Confrécourt, north of Soissons. Known as the 'Chapel of Father Doncoeur', this is one of many spectacular carvings in the region's soft chalk and limestone geology.

Chapter 6

THE SOCIAL WORLDS OF TRENCH ART

The true significance of Trench Art has lain hidden for over eighty years, concealed beneath a mass of military history, social history, and literary works which have dominated our understanding of the Great War and its aftermath. In an attempt to recover some of Trench Art's historical significance, and to understand what it can tell us of the ordinary people who made, bought, and used it, anthropology must be our guide.

We can attempt to go further – to understand both the detail and the generality of Trench Art by providing the objects and those concerned with them with a context. Each piece is more than just an object made of a particular material or shaped into a specific form – it resonates in distinctive ways with the lives and experiences of the person who made it, and those who came, and continue to come, into contact with it.

Anthropologists see objects as possessing important and variable social meanings beyond (as well as including) the original purpose for which they were made. By studying these different meanings – the changing values and attitudes attached to Trench Art by different people over time – we can explore what may be called the 'social lives' of these objects. In other words, a piece of Trench Art embodies the ideas and emotions of the person who makes it, and of those whose hands it passes through up to the present day. While some will always regard such items as the junk of war, others will see objects for sale or barter; many will find themselves repelled by the very idea of Trench Art, but some will be brought to the verge of tears as they recall poignant memories associated with a particular object. Trench Art exercises a powerful pull on our emotions, as it has the potential to distil the variety of human reactions to the experiences of war.

The world is full of things people make and these things quietly shape our experience of life. While the individual item of Trench Art remains the same today as it was eighty years ago, the passage of time and of generations means that it will always elicit different responses according to who is looking at it and where they are in history. As our piece of Trench Art travels through time, and is handed from soldier to wife, mother to child, grandparent to grandchild, and, perhaps, eventually sold on to an anonymous buyer, it follows a unique path through the world. Tracking this path as it cuts across the lives of many different people helps us to build a biography of the piece.

We all, to a degree, define who we are by the relationship we have to the things we choose to make, buy or display in our homes. In this sense, Trench Art is a hitherto untapped resource for exploring the lives of all who came into contact with it between 1914 and 1939 – soldiers, refugees, prisoners of war, internees, and the families left without a husband, father or brother. In this chapter will be explored some of the wider issues associated with Trench Art which, in my opinion, offer new ways of looking not just at the objects, but at what really matters – the people, aspects of whose lives in the tumult of war it so uniquely embodies.

Fig. 6.1a: Devastation to property and farming land on the Somme. Typical of the devastion wrought by the Great War.

Fig. 6.1b: Artillery barages produced many evocative and symbolic images of the clash between industrialized war and nature, as in this photograph of a shell lodged in a shattered tree.

Landscapes of Metal

As a special kind of artefact, Trench Art conjures memories of mens' experiences in landscapes of war so appalling they have become etched into the historical consciousness of the twentieth century. The name Trench Art, although misleading, is nevertheless evocative of experiences which mixed together soldiers, shells, death and comradeship in trench-scarred landscapes which have become archetypal images of the Great War and which are typified by the Western Front.

Despite the largely static character of trench warfare, Western Front battlefields were spiritually unstable places. The bucolic fields of Picardy, Artois and Flanders had once been tilled for crops but were now 'drenched with hot metals', the ground shattered, pastoral settings transformed into lunar landscapes of endless craters, barbed wire, devastated buildings and blasted trees. A rural idyll had become unrecognizable wasteland with dead bodies, ammunition and putrefaction extending from the English Channel to the Swiss border, and, in horrific concentration, between Ieper (Ypres) and Verdun.

The relationship of soldiers – and in a different way the battlefield pilgrims who followed them after 1918 – with the metals of war was highly ambiguous. This is hardly surprising when it is considered that almost three-quarters of wounds sustained were caused by shellfire.

Fig. 6.2: Trench life in a 'quiet' sector of the Western Front in the early summer of 1915. Men of the Territorial Army, 1/5th York and Lancaster Regiment, get acclimatized to living conditions under the eyes of the enemy. Periods of inactivity and resulting boredom doubtless gave rise to the creative pastimes. Seated soldier holds a small mallet of the kind commonly used to make Trench Art.

Fig. 6.2a: Industry at the Front. French soldiers recuperating metal in the spirit of improvisation that led to many Trench Art masterpieces.

Soldiers were exposed to hitherto unimaginable quantities of bombs, mortars, shrapnel, bullets and gas – a hail of death which they were expected either to endure in their dugouts, or advance through during an attack. Many personal accounts vividly recall such terrible experiences. In the papers of Miss Dorothy Scoles we read the account of an unnamed soldier: 'Showers of lead flying about & big big shells its an unearthy (sic) sight to see them drop in amongst human beings. The cries are terrible ...'.

After battle or bombardment, the land was strewn with the detritus of industrialized war – spent shells, cooling shrapnel and unexploded ordnance which could (and did) explode unexpectedly, adding further to the toll of death and mutilating injury. Interspersed with this chaos of materials were the equally shattered remains of the soldiers themselves. In 1917 in the Ypres Salient, Sergeant H.E. May of the Gordon Highlanders observed that the battlefield,

Fig. 6.3: Trench bottom littered with German dead.

'... was a vision indescribable in its naked horror. Pieces of metal that once were cannon; and, if good Krupp steel had been so shattered, what of the humans who served the steel ? Heads, legs, arms, trunks, pieces of rotting flesh, skulls that grinned hideously, bones cleaned by exposure, lay about in hopeless riot.'

Fig. 6.3a: Temporary battle-zone altar made of German artillery shells and used for religious services.

The intensity of such physical and psychological experiences led not only to shell shock but also to breaking the mould of everyday experiences inherited from life before the war. In the trenches, dugouts and on the battlefields, soldiers found they often could see very little. Trench life was characterized by a thin strip of sky visible from beneath the parapet, and dugouts were dark and dingy places. During battle, no mans land was a miasma of smoke, gas, blasted earth, and craters. In other words, the dominance of vision had been undermined by the technology of war. In its place, soldiers developed intuition, and their senses of smell, touch and hearing. New meanings were attached to the lights, sounds, smells, tastes and vibrations of war on such a massive scale. Such vivid impressions are a feature of the most striking war memoirs and poetry by such authors as Edmund Blunden, Siegfried Sassoon, Robert Graves and Wilfred Owen.

An indication of these heightened sensory experiences is provided by Private Alexander Paterson of the Glasgow Highlanders who,

Fig. 6.4: Temporary battlefield grave with a Trench Art marker cross of artillery shell cases and bullet cartridges.

during his time on the Western Front, developed,

'... an expert knowledge of all the strange sounds and smells of warfare, ignorance of which may mean death to a man who is not quick to apprehend their meaning. My hearing was attuned to every kind of explosion from the hacking cough of bombs to the metallic clanging of 5.9 shells bursting in re-echoing valleys. My nostrils were quick to detect a whiff of gas or to diagnose the menace of a corpse disinterred at an interval of months.'

In such conditions, a sense of hopelessness overwhelmed many soldiers, leading them to believe that every incoming shell was inscribed with a man's name. In the soldiers' imagination, such a fate might be averted by having one's name already en-graved on a talismanic bullet – an especially poign-ant kind of category 1 Trench Art. The vast quantities of shells fired, reinforced such fatalism on an almost daily basis. In the preliminary bombardment for the Third Battle of Ypres in July 1917, the Royal Artillery alone fired 4,283,550 rounds, and, during the whole battle, the Germans discharged some 18,000,000 shells. Under these conditions, front line soldiers had somehow to contrive a 'normal' everyday existence in landscapes whose terrible sights and associations supplied a 'free' and inexhaustible supply of raw materials for metal Trench Art. These associations guaranteed that any finished objects would be deeply ambiguous – embodying emotions and experiences which could never be explained or even mentioned to their families back home.

Fig. 6.4: The soldier's ultimate talisman – 'the bullet with your name on it'. This one is engraved 'Frank'. Was its owner a Great War survivor?

For Catholic French soldiers, bomb-shattered villages, with their ruined churches and shattered images of Christ, were places of spiritual unease. Such feelings found physical expression in another kind of talismanic Trench Art known as the 'bullet-crucifix', typically made from several bullet cartridges, and a figure of Christ soldered onto the front. These miniatures were in turn associated with the pre-war popularity of roadside Calvaries and which, because of the miraculous survival of some, achieved near mythic status among soldiers. 'Crucifix Corner' on the Somme was perhaps the most famous of these – its rusty, bullet-blasted remains are still visible today. Bullet-crucifixes were carried by soldiers during the war (and have been found on battlefields) but also became popular among battlefield pilgrims and tourists after 1918 when they were decorated also with regimental badges and small memorial plaques (typically carrying an image of the Menin Gate at Ieper {Ypres}) and were sometimes mounted on a tripod of bullets.

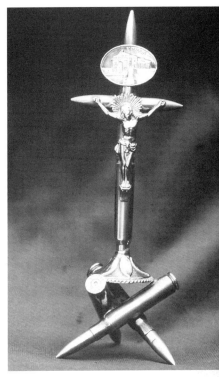

Fig. 6.6: Bullet-crucifix on tripod of German Mauser bullets. The memorial plaque showing the Menin Gate at Ieper (Ypres) dates it to 1927 onwards, indicating it was made as a souvenir for the battlefield pilgrims and tourists.

After the war, the killing fields were transformed into landscapes of remembrance – places where pilgrims and the curious could explore their own personal and cultural identities and come to terms with what the war meant to them. Along the Western Front and at Gallipoli especially, but also in Italy, Macedonia and Mesopotamia, the sheer number of the dead together with the industrialized nature of the conflict meant that 'The Missing' dominated the landscape as a

Fig. 6.7: Memorial Cross on the site of Maltz Horn Farm near Guillemont on the Somme.

Fig. 6.8: The Menin Gate Memorial to the Missing, Ieper (Ypres), Belgium.

spiritual presence whose only physical existence lay in their names etched into the stone of huge memorials such as Thiepval on the Somme, and Tyne Cot and the Menin Gate in the Ypres Salient.

Those who visited the battlefields and their associated cemeteries and memorials were not simply tramping over the places of past conflict. They were also travelling back through time, through memories, and associating themselves with places attached to the dead. Battlefield guidebooks, war poetry, innumerable memoirs and regimental war diaries added a poignant texture to these experiences. Although they themselves were forever separated from the experiences of battle, they authenticated their experiences by buying souvenirs of their visit. In this way, as David Lloyd says in his book *Battlefield Tourism*, they were able to take home a tangible link with the spirit of their dead loved ones.

Those who purchased such items presumably did so for a variety of reasons, perhaps as souvenirs of their visits, as personal acts of worship to the memory of the deceased, and maybe also as a display of solidarity and empathy with local people for whom their loved ones had sacrificed their lives and whose terrible deprivations were everywhere apparent. It is certainly true that, for the governments and returning refugees of Belgium and France, battlefield tourism was a major factor in rebuilding their shattered economies.

Such instances illustrate a wider point about the connections of Trench Art objects. Different kinds of Trench Art did not stand alone for the soldier, refugee or battlefield pilgrim – rather they joined together with shattered buildings, devastated landscapes, human bodies (often left unburied for years) and memories, to forge the experience of 'being in' a landscape. Trench Art souvenirs embodied these feelings and carried the past through the present and into the future.

Fig. 6.9: The Australian, John (Barney) Hines, known as the 'Souvenir King' and branded a barbarian by the Kaiser when he saw this photograph. *Courtesy of Australian War Memorial*

Fig. 6.9a: Trophies taken from German trenches at Vimy Ridge and Messines.

Trench Art as Souvenirs

One of the most intriguing aspects of Trench Art, and one which is forever linked to the human experience of battlefield landscapes, is its identification as a distinctive kind of souvenir – in fact two kinds of souvenir, one tied to the conditions of war, the other to the often poignant circumstances of the following peace.

All kinds of Trench Art may be considered to have been souvenirs at one time, both for soldiers and civilians. For soldiers and service personnel during the war, Trench Art items, especially those of metal, were part of a much wider phenomenon of acquiring objects associated with battle, either by purchase, barter, making it oneself or collecting it during or just after a battle. The ambiguity of souvenir hunting during the war is apparent in the coining of the term 'souveneering', which

Fig. 6.9b: Some souvenirs brought home for display as captured booty at a Regimental HQ in South Yorkshire in 1916.

often was a thinly veiled euphemism for stealing or looting anything from an artillery shell case to a dead soldier's personal effects, or a fragment of stained glass from the ruins of the Cloth Hall at Ieper (Ypres). On 8 March 1916, Captain P.H. Rawson wrote home, 'Has that Bosche button arrived ? Mind you don't lose it as I cut it off with my own hands, the only real hun I have been close to and an awful brute he looked too.'

Collecting souvenirs was often a risky business. There are many contemporary accounts of soldiers taking foolhardy risks in order to acquire that unusual trophy – the danger itself probably adding to the value of the piece. So commonplace was it for a soldier to be killed or wounded while 'souveneering' that it was often reported almost nonchalantly. In The War the Infantry Knew 1914-1919, Captain J.C. Dunn relates several cases gleaned from eyewitness accounts. On the night of 29 October 1914, a German officer had been killed in British trenches and was found to be carrying a French revolver dated 1875 – quite possibly one he had 'souveneered' himself from a dead Frenchman. At the tail end of the war, one of Dunn's informants tells

Fig. 6.9c: An official request for soldiers to salvage munitions and other items.

how, in September 1918, Signallers Napper and Jones had been killed near Sailly-Saillisel on the Somme, and how 'Napper was found dead, bayoneted in several places; he was a great souvenir hunter.'

The majority of these 'souveneered' pieces were original whole items, such as bullets, lumps of shrapnel, buttons, regimental badges and miscellaneous bits of military equipment. Some have extraordinary stories attached, such as the piece of shrapnel from the first shell to welcome a soldier newly arrived in France in October 1915 and which he found in his pocket.

These items could be made into Trench Art by soldiers (i.e. category 1a) as in the case of the Trench Art clock made by Sapper Pearl described before, or a piece of the dome from the Dardanelles Lighthouse adorned with a Turkish crescent and star and dated 1915.

Alternatively, they could be taken home to be made up into a mounted trophy (i.e. category 3). Often, such objects remained in their 'raw' state as simple souvenirs of war and never became Trench Art at all. In all three cases, the souvenirs carried memories and associations of the momentous, and often life-and-death, experiences of those who acquired them.

While soldiers might keep, barter or sell such items, battlefield visitors, both during and after the war usually took them home to keep. For civilians, as for soldiers, souvenir hunting often verged on obssession. As early as 1914, *The War Illustrated* published photographs of civilians searching for German bullets in the grass, with the prescient comment that, 'Souvenir hunting has become quite an industry where the fire of battle has raged, and it is certain

Fig. 6.10: Trench Art souvenirs for sale in front of shell damaged Reims cathedral during the 1930s.

Fig. 6.11: Elaborately decorated brass souvenir letter holder dated '1919'.

54

POPULAR SOUVENIRS

CAPTURED

Jardiniere (8″ Howitzer

GERMAN CARTRIDGE CASES

TRANSFORMED INTO ATTRACTIVE UTILITIES.

Pedestal
(5.9″ Gun & 8″ Howitzer)

COLLECTED on the Western F
during the war, they are unique
useful, and are the most popular of
Souvenirs. Strongly constructed of
best brass, they are practically everlast
Having most of their weight in the I
they are not easily overbalanced, and
therefore ideal for the display of I
bunches of flowers or gum tips. They
specially lacquered and retain indefin
the highly-polished finish in which they
delivered.

For prices and particulars apply to

AUSTRALIAN WAR MEMORIAL MUSEUM.

Exhibition Building,

SYDNEY.

Fig. 6.12: Post-war Australian advertisement for Trench Art souvenirs made from German artillery shell cases.

Fig. 6.13: Member of the Belgian Army's bomb disposal unit removing an unexploded artillery shell from a farm near Ieper (Ypres).

that the traffic in war souvenirs will flourish in the years to come when battlefields are the haunt of summer tourists.'

During the war, the making of Trench Art from battlefield debris quickly became a cottage industry, the finished products being sold first to soldiers and then to battlefield pilgrims and visitors. Such was the demand for all types of souvenir, that tourists were not averse to 'souveneering' from their own army during official tours of the trenches. One serviceman satirized such events in a poem:

> 'Ladies and Gentlemen this is High Wood
> You are requested kindly not to touch or take away
> the comp'ny's property as souvenirs
> you'll find we have on sale a large variety all
> guaranteed...'

The hunt for souvenirs, whether Trench Art or miscellaneous battlefield items, continues today, and in many respects it remains a dangerous undertaking. While buying Trench Art in militaria fairs and flea markets entails no risk (apart from sometimes inflated prices and the increasing hazard of fakes) battlefield souvenirs are a different matter. Today, in an average year, the Somme yields some 90 tonnes of dangerously volatile 'hardware' – known as the 'iron harvest' – which still causes fatalities among farmers, those in search of first-hand souvenirs, and even the professional bomb disposal teams of the French and Belgian armies. In the fields around Ieper (Ypres), up to 250,000 kgs of such materials are recovered in a year – so much that the Belgian Army disposes of it in controlled explosions twice or three times a day. It is estimated that it will take at least one hundred years to clear the majority of unexploded shells still in the ground.

Trench Art in the Home

Trench Art souvenirs of all kinds, especially those made of metal, had a renewed if poignant significance after the war. Indeed, as we have seen, sub-category 2 b items – those made during the inter-war years – were by far the largest quantity

Fig. 6.14: Trench Art table lamp made from an artillery shell case, engraved 'Champagne'.

Fig. 6.15: Early post-war temporary wooden house built for returning Belgian refugees to the battlefield outside Ypres. Several decorated artillery shell cases stand on the table and window sill.

made. As large numbers of the bereaved and the curious made their way to the old battlefields and the increasing number of associated memorials that were being built, they bought Trench Art as mementoes and took them home as heart-rending souvenirs of their visits. Such activities gave Trench Art objects a new lease of life, one whose significance and meanings differed in many important respects from objects made and sold during the war, which had tended to resonate for the soldier rather than the bereaved.

When Trench Art objects were placed in the home they played a variable and still little understood role in the working out of personal emotions for their owners. The deciding factor appears to have been whether or not the household's menfolk had returned from the war. Some items which originally had been sent home with pride as

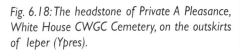

Fig. 6.17: Memorial stitching to Private A Pleasance, East Yorkshire Regiment, killed in action 21 September 1915. This piece was bought in England and taken to Ypres, where coincidently, Private Pleasance is buried in White House CWGC Cemetery.

Fig. 6.18: The headstone of Private A Pleasance, White House CWGC Cemetery, on the outskirts of Ieper (Ypres).

souvenirs by soldiers later became symbols of loss for the family when the soldier did not return. If the soldier had returned, then such objects may have served as a memento of war service which expressed personal pride and relief in their achievement and survival. For these men, Trench Art recalled memories of deeply formative experiences in the forging and loss of comradeship.

A remarkable insight into the play of emotions and attitudes in these situations is provided by Colonel N.B. Chaffers who wrote home to his mother on 19 September 1915.

'By now you may have received two shell cartridges, I asked one of the men in my coy [company] to take them home, and post them on to

Fig. 6.18: The only early post-war (1920s) wooden house to survive in Ieper (Ypres). It's decoration of wartime memorabilia and Trench Art Shell cases was once commonplace.

you. They are quite safe, as they are only the empty cartridges from which the shell has been fired, and when engraved they make quite nice souvenirs. ... If the maids have time they might clean them with brass polish. I should suggest putting them on the hall mantelpiece. The work was done by a French tommy from whom I bought them.'

Trench Art created a world of shared experiences, emotions, and hopes. It found individual expression through its use to decorate and personalize the home – itself an extension of an individual's personality. Like all ornaments, it altered physical space, rearranged the surroundings and accomodated itself to the changed

Fig. 6.19: Photograph frame made from scrap brass and aluminium, and engraved with 'Souvenir de Emile Larnou'.

emotional atmosphere of a home without a husband, father, brother or son. Trench Art in the home was a way of linking the desolated individual with the wider community of bereaved, through shared displays of objects and also ensured that memories were always just a glance away.

For the bereaved, placing a metal letter-opener, bullet-crucifix, or pair of polished shells on the mantelpiece, in the hallway or on a bedside dresser – perhaps next to a photograph of the deceased – was a constant visual reminder of the loved one. There was also a very sensual dimension to such activities. Many Trench Art souvenirs were made of brass, a metal which tarnishes quickly. It is almost certain that the arrival of such items in the home gave rise to a domestic routine of cleaning and polishing, and that, in many cases, this probably had therapeutic effects for the bereaved. Sometimes such activities became an obsessive compulsion, with the result that decades of polishing erased the original decoration and inscription almost completely. It is ironic that such faintly inscribed pieces today fetch smaller prices because of their almost invisible decoration, yet it was these which probably were most valued by their original owners. It was also ironic that objects made originally for killing should be tended so lovingly.

For some women, the sense of grief must also have been tinged with ambiguity. Those who had worked in munitions factories and who had lost a husband, father, brother or sweetheart were caught in a paradox. For them, shells and bullets were simultaneously a manifestation of

Fig. 6.20: Photograph frame made from wood from HMS Furious and with the ship's name simply engraved onto a brass plate.

Fig. 6.21: Drawing of an almost erased design engraved onto a 1915 American 75mm artillery shell case. It shows a shell about to hit a German soldier with the inscription 'Fritz in Fits'.
Author copyright with acknowledgement to Roxanne Saunders

their economic independence and positive contribution to the war effort, yet, when transformed into Trench Art, the same objects became a constant reminder of their loss.

It may be that the poignancy surrounding the presence of Trench Art ornaments in the home, and the rituals which came from them, were a purely or mainly British phenomenon. However, it seems likely that in Canada, Australia, New Zealand, France and possibly Italy, similar activities took place. In Germany, private ways in which the living reconciled themselves with the dead and resolved their sense of loss may have been somewhat different. It appears that German homes often had a little memorial shrine made up of a photograph of the deceased which was draped in mourning at appropriate times. For some Germans at least, buying and then displaying polished Trench Art was a morbid if not a barbarian act – a fact which highlights the difference in cultural attitudes towards Trench Art objects and between national ways of remembering the dead.

The capacity of Trench Art objects in the home to represent, release, or stimulate personal memories was not restricted to those who had fought and survived, or who had lost a loved one. In the remarkable book by Marian Wenzel and John Cornish, *Auntie Mabel's War*, we have an account of a nurse who served with the Scottish Women's Hospital in Northern France and the Balkans during the Great War. At the beginning of the book, we are confronted with a unique insight into how memories can be triggered by a Trench Art souvenir which had become a household ornament.

The object in question is a French 75mm artillery shell case, punch-decorated with flowers, and bearing an inscription 'Ambulance 12/14, Soissons, 1918'. It was the presence of this shell which 'released' the memory of Auntie Mabel in the mind of her niece, Mrs Turner, and led to a flood of recollections which became the book. As she told Marian Wenzel,

> *'Yes, that thing by the fireplace with the flowers on it is really a shell case. ... She brought that back from France for her parents; I thought it was an awfully morbid thing. ... It got to Granny's house and then it came here. ... I often look at it and wonder how many men its shell killed.'*

After the war, many families had Trench Art objects on display in the home. By virtue of having been worked and decorated they were

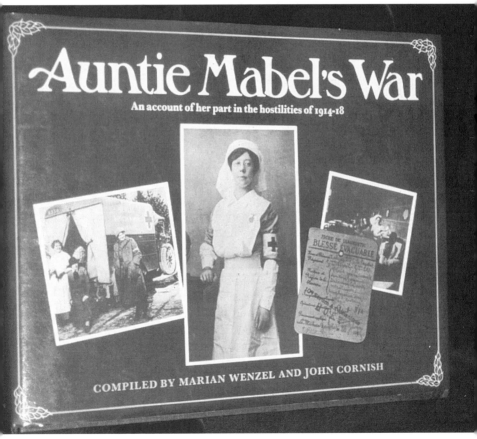

Fig. 6.22: Auntie Mabel's War *by Marian Wenzel and John Cornish.*
Courtesy of Marian Wenzel

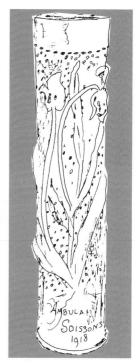

Fig. 6.23: Marian Wenzel's original drawing of Auntie Mabel's Trench Art souvenir/fireplace ornament.
Courtesy of Marian Wenzel

Fig. 6.24: Auntie Mabel's shell.
Author copyright with acknowledgement to Marian Wenzel

somehow more civilized than raw mementoes which were nothing other than battlefield debris. Trench Art bore the traces of human creativity amidst inhuman destruction. Perhaps, when displayed in the hallway, bedroom or living room, they went some way to healing the pain, to stand in as it were for a loved one who would never return.

Such must have been the case for the Goss family, the inventors of Heraldic Porcelain. Both sons, Raymond and Dick, had gone to war and in August 1915 just outside Ieper (Ypres), a shell exploded killing Raymond outright and wounding Dick in the shoulder. Ironically, Raymond had previously sent home a brass shell case to his father as a souvenir. After Raymond's death the family had it inscribed 'French '75' Shell Case sent home by Sec. Lt. Raymond G.G. Goss 1/5th N. Staffs. Reg. (1915 killed near Hill 60 in Flanders August 1915).'

Across Europe, and beyond, countless families struggled to understand what the war had done to them physically and spiritually. In their attempts to come to terms with their tragedies, the bereaved tried to control their emotions, to enclose their grief in a way which allowed them to respect and remember the dead yet go on with their lives. In many households, this psychological balancing act was expressed in the things with which the bereaved surrounded themselves. It is difficult not to see Trench Art souvenir-ornaments as playing a unique role in these painful coming to terms.

Trench Art as Art

The broken, fragmented world which the Great War produced found its miniature in Trench Art – portable pieces of war made into whole items of peace. Unlike simple unaltered mementoes, Trench Art was an expression of the human instinct to create – ironically here – from the residue of the equally powerful impulse to destroy. Metal Trench Art may be seen as a three dimensional manifestation of the oft made point that the Great War's grotesque nature was not denied but rather aestheticised. In particular, the strange conglomerations of shells and bullets, and wood and bone, were the embodiment of Modernism. As Samuel Hynes has observed in *A War Imagined*, '... a Modernist method that before the war had seemed violent and distorting was seen to be realistic on the Western Front. Modernism had not changed, but reality had.'

Trench Art can be seen as a physical representation of widely held post-war attitudes concerning ideas of dislocation and fragmentation in societies across Europe especially, but elsewhere too. The war seemed a 'gap' in history where time itself was ruptured by a conflict so intense that it shattered not just human bodies, families and social relationships, but wider European beliefs about the nature of society, civilization, art and scientific progress as well. The twentieth century was born here, and it was a painful birth. In a memorable statement, Camille Mauclair said, 'The war has figuratively but powerfully dug a trench between yesterday's ideas and those of today ... We have all been thrown outside ourselves...'.

Against the background of such events, much Trench Art embodied the confusions of the war as ambiguous weapons and scrap transformed into ambiguous art for ambiguous times. Many of the metal objects in particular were made from parts of weapons which were still recognizable as such – objects of death and maiming put together to create art.

The influence of Trench Art on the development of the avant-garde and Modernism appears so far to have escaped the notice of art historians. Yet the evidence is suggestive and there for all to see. Perhaps predictably, metal Trench Art is again to the fore in this. The Cubist painter Fernand Léger believed that Cubism was especially appropriate to portray life in the trenches, as in his paintings Soldier with a Pipe (1916) and The Card Players (1917). The whole idea of destruction as creation, and Cubism's unique ability to capture this seeming paradox by marrying together modern forms with wartime subjects, could equally be applied to many items of Trench Art. Some kinds of Trench Art appear as three dimensional Cubism, and many Cubist paintings seem almost to be two dimensional representations of certain kinds of Trench Art.

What emerges from this brief but wide ranging account is a glimpse of the many ways in which Trench Art intersected with peoples lives, during and after the war, and of its influence on diverse aspects of European culture. It is these wider perspectives which make Great War Trench Art significant for the history of the twentieth century – a century defined by war, its objects and its tragic aftermath.

Fig. 6.25:The Drinking shell. It seems as if every aspect of a soldier's battle-zone life was defined by artillery shells.

Chapter 7

TRENCH ART TODAY

The ideas and values which Great War Trench Art represented faded with the coming of the Second World War. There were several reasons for this. Many soldiers who survived the First World War were killed in the Second, and were remembered for the conflict which killed them, not the one they survived. After 1945, the British public was much concerned with mourning a new generation of the dead which this time included many civilians as well as soldiers. In the Second World War, unlike the First, death was not distanced by geography, but came to the towns and homes of ordinary people particularly in London and southern England. As a consequence of this, much time and effort was directed towards reconstructing towns and cities which had been bombed by the German Luftwaffe.

In addition, after 1945, memories of the dead of both wars were squeezed together in acts of joint remembrance which further distanced many from the unique and distinctive features of the Great War. The name also changed. What had been known as 'The Great War' in a sense was devalued by becoming 'The First World War'. Even the stony surfaces of the country's war memorials were altered as inscriptions were modified or added in order to include the names of the more recent dead. One result of these changes was that the Great War no longer had a monopoly on peoples' emotions – a fact which all but guaranteed that the post-1945 period would be very different from the years which followed the November 1918 Armistice.

After 1945, Trench Art of the Great War and inter-war years appears to have become increasingly unfashionable and anachronistic. It belonged to the war before the last war, and seemed to embody notions of unquestioning patriotism and 'glorious' (if tragic) sacrifice which characterized a kind of society which was fast disappearing. Given expression by battlefield pilgrimages and the unveiling of commemorative memorials at home and abroad, Trench Art may also have recalled memories of the inter-war hopes for a peaceful future which had been shattered in 1939. For many, Trench Art pieces were among the definitive objects of the Great War and now seemed alienated and largely irrelevant to a modern future, which was to be based on consumerism and the psychology, sometimes hysteria, surrounding the conflict that never was – the Cold War.

For these reasons and others, the 1950s and early 1960s saw the low point of public interest in the Great War and in visits to its battlefields and memorials, from Gallipoli to the old Western Front. Across France and Belgium and probably elsewhere, metal Trench Art pieces were worth more as scrap than as objects of Great War history. How many masterpieces disappeared during these years we will never know. At the same time, other kinds of Trench Art, like embroidered postcards, carved wood and items of beadwork, seemingly left the category of Trench Art and became instead collectable objects in wider spheres of collecting. Such pieces were now curious and anonymous additions for those who collected or traded only in postcards, textiles or beadwork. However, developing technologies and the human capacity for remembrance were about to combine and give Trench Art a new lease of life.

In 1964, commemorations of the fiftieth anniversary of the start of the Great War were highlighted by the broadcasting of several television histories – notably the BBC's monumental *The Great War*. With a television in almost every home, public awareness of the Great War was probably deeper and more widespread during the mid-sixties than at any time since the war itself. The impact was immediate. By the early 1970s there were some 50,000 visitors a year to the old battlefields, and, by 1974, this had increased to 250,000. Throughout the 1980s and 1990s, there was a mushrooming of specialist travel companies to cater for the demand. This was reinforced by a similar increase in the number of societies dedicated to one or other aspect of the Great War, such as the founding of the 'Western Front Association' in 1980 – each of which organized its own battlefield tours. An unexpected boost to the burgeoning numbers of visitors was given by the inclusion of the First World War and associated fieldtrips in the National Curriculum of the British educational system and which led to many coachloads of school children visiting the Western Front – something their parents, born in the 1950s, had seldom done. As in the inter-war years, this explosion of battlefield tourists led to an increasing interest in souvenirs, many of which were, and continue to be, examples of Trench Art, some original, and others less so.

In France and Belgium especially, Trench Art objects are sold today alongside a miscellany of other Great War objects, such as defused

Fig. 7.1: Schoolchildren on a trip to the battlefields, June 2000.

bullets, grenades, buttons, medals, officers' whistles and pieces of uniforms. Some of these inevitably are bought by great grandchildren and great-nephews and nieces of old soldiers. The result is that Trench Art souvenirs have a new lease of life. Trench Art today also has a parallel existence in the burgeoning militaria trade. Most Trench Art items have lost the subtleties of meaning with which they were once endowed through their connections to memories of the war and inter-war years. Stripped of their original associations, they are left now with only highly relative notions of wildly fluctuating commercial values. Today, such qualities as fineness of form, completeness, distinctiveness and shiny appearance have replaced once poignant memories and resonances.

Along with these new values, often comes a raft of anecdotal information concerning individual pieces. This information is offered as associated memories bestowed on those who buy or are given the objects – whether dealer, private collector or museum curator. Sometimes such information is a kind of 'value-adding' proof of authenticity, other times, perhaps, a final closing of memory's door.

Fig. 7.2: Genuine First World War exploded shell Trench Art with ceramic Madonna.

Fig. 7.3: An example of replica Trench Art; this comprises an original Great War shell, plastic Madonna and NATO issue rounds.

Fig. 7.5: Car boot collection of Trench Art on sale at an English militaria fair.

Fig. 7.4: Battlefield souvenirs for sale on the Somme. Grenade and fuze-cap sectioned to show internal mechanism.

Much significant information is thus passed on in a random fashion on the back of a commercial transaction not dissimilar to the original selling of the object between 1914 and 1939. Many items however have become anonymous. House clearances and car-boot sales often discover and pass on objects which, like orphans, have become forever detached from the associations of their original owners and families.

There is now a new kind of ambiguity surrounding Trench Art. Dealers, collectors and market-stall holders are often unsure how to describe or value such objects. Some militaria dealers regard Trench Art as a waste of 'good clean shells and bullets', while others see them as interesting objects from an eighty-five year old war. Every dealer and collector will offer a different view on the state of the Trench Art market. Some believe that Trench Art is so abundant that the market is 'flat', while others see it as increasingly rare and accruing in value. The truth probably lies somewhere in between. It is certainly the case that some examples – especially the metal forms – are being faked, if that is the right word. Original First World War shell cases are being rather badly engraved, and bullet pens made from recent NATO ordnance are sometimes sold as mementoes and other times passed off as Great War originals. On Occasion, particularly fine pieces are stolen from museums.

In Belgium and France especially, there is much rivalry between collectors who have amassed often stunning private collections. In the course of my own research, it has been necessary to wait upwards of a year to overcome the natural reluctance of some collectors to allow an outsider to visit their homes. Building a network of contacts and sometimes sworn to secrecy, it has often seemed as if my investigation concerned an illicit trade in diamonds or drugs rather than base metal artefacts from the First World War. The arguments, disputes, deceptions and sometimes violence which characterize the rivalry between serious collectors, and which goes beyond Trench Art into general militaria, add an unusual and peculiarly human twist to the continuing and ever changing social lives of these objects.

Trench Art and Museums

At the moment, Trench Art objects are undervalued by museums in many parts of the world. They are still considered the curious, if sometimes astonishingly ingenious, ephemera of war, lacking any aesthetic or artistic impact or emotional appeal. Almost certainly this will change as curators increasingly begin to see these objects as a

Fig. 7.7: A treasure trove of of Trench Art stacked on shelves in the storeroom of the Historial de la Grande Guerre, Peronne, France.

unique historical resource, and one whose educational potential via exhibitions, information packs, and associated hands-on activities for adults and children alike, is as yet largely untapped.

Currently, there is only a handful of Trench Art objects on display in major museums. London's Imperial War Museum has a small selection on public view, though retains a much larger collection in its storerooms. Almost all the items have been donated and today the museum's curators turn away most items offered, accepting only the most distinctive or unusual pieces. The National Army Museum in Chelsea has only recently begun acquiring Trench Art. As yet there is little on display but its collections include some fine pieces. The same is true for the Australian War Memorial in Canberra which houses Sapper Pearl's collection and a number of other excellent examples of the genre.

In Belgium, at Ieper's recently revamped 'In Flanders Fields Museum', there are less items on display than previously but those which can be seen are magnificent pieces. In the already mentioned Streeksmuseum in nearby Zonnebeke is a small display of Trench Art objects originally collected for a 1972 exhibition, and featuring the Versavel toolkit. France's premier First World War museum, the Historial de la Grande Guerre has a small number of striking pieces on view – an English Tommy's helmet painted with a landscape scene, and an elaborately baroque artillery shell case decorated with bullets and made into a clock. During the First World War, in the dark days of 1915, there were two exhibitions of Trench Art held at the *Salles du Jeu de Paume des Tuileries* in Paris – the first having a selection board which boasted such luminaries as Renoir, Rodin and Lalique.

Fig. 7.6: Rare display of Trench Art in a British museum. It is part of the exhibition 'Transformations: The Art of Recycling', at the Pitt Rivers Museum, Oxford.

A hitherto untapped resource for the study of Trench Art is the large number of regimental

Fig. 7.8: Magnificent Trench Art clock in the café-museum at Hill 62, Sanctuary Wood, outside Ieper (Ypres), Belgium.

museums throughout the United Kingdom and beyond. A two year survey conducted by the author revealed a treasure trove of objects sometimes well documented, occasionally on display, but almost never studied. Such items include a hand bell cast from part of a larger bell from Ieper (Ypres) cathedral in the museum of the King's Own Royal Regiment (Lancaster), shell cases made into Royal Artillery Service

Fig. 7.9: Detail of the clock face of the second of the Trench Art clocks at Sanctuary Wood café-museum.

Dress Uniform caps in the Royal Artillery Regimental Museum, a table lighter made from a German shell cap found at Touquet near Bois Grenier in February 1915 in the Royal Welch Fusiliers Museum, and a collection of colourful and intricately worked handkerchief love tokens made by resting soldiers and now held in the museum of The Duke of Cornwall's Light Infantry.

Of particular interest is a bronze German shell case picked up in France just before the war's end by Captain A.S.C. Fothergill of the 2/6th Battalion of the Royal Regiment of Fusiliers (Lancashire) on which are engraved the names of fallen officers and other ranks and the battalion's war service. This trophy is displayed at battalion reunions, a history-laden object which encapsulates personal memories and regimental pride.

While Trench Art does not yet have a high profile in national or regimental museums, it does have a special place in a kind of public display unique to the old Western Front and which probably has its origins in the inter-war years battlefield pilgrimages described above. The café-museums which are to be found near Ieper (Ypres) in Belgium and Albert on the Somme possess some of the finest public displays of Great War Trench Art anywhere in the world. Some are recently established, others have changed hands, and many have disappeared, but in general they follow a long tradition of catering for battlefield visitors of all persuasions.

On the infamous Menin Road just outside Ieper (Ypres), lies the Hooge Crater café-museum, which incorporates an old memorial chapel to the soldiers who died in the Ypres Salient. It stands opposite the CWGC Cemetery of the same name. Inside the café is a different kind of memorial - shelf after shelf stacked with a seemingly endless variety of decorated, corsetted, and brightly polished artillery shell cases in what must be the single most impressive collection of such objects on public display anywhere. Standing shoulder to shoulder, row on row, these shiny regiments of shells testify to the extraordinary skills of their makers, and poignantly symbolize the terrible loss of human life that took place on this spot especially between 1915 and 1916.

While the café is dominated by Trench Art shells, the adjoining museum exhibits some of the more unusual and well-preserved smaller items. There is a superb Trench Art model of a German Taube monoplane, matchbox covers (one engraved with a soldier's name), a shrapnel letter-opener, writing equipment, and embroidered tobacco pouches. Giving a sense of time-and-place is a dazzling display of First World War militaria, munitions, and scene-setting reconstructions.

Nearby, at the Sanctuary Wood CWGC Cemetery, is another café-museum with a display of decorated shell cases along the window sills, fireplace, and on shelves behind the bar. Modern Trench Art pieces - key-rings and bullet-pens - are sold as souvenirs in much the same way as they were during the inter-war years. Pride of place at the Sanctuary Wood museum belongs to two remarkable large clocks made from

Fig. 7.10: Hooge Crater Museum on the Menin Road outside Ieper (Ypres), Belgium, in 2000. The museum has the most comprehensive collection of Trench Art shell cases anywhere along the old Western Front.

wood, artillery shell cases and bullet cartridges. There are many stories concerning these clocks, some of which date them to the years before the war, while others attribute them to the inter-war years.

In France, on the Somme, at the small village of Pozières, just outside Albert on the Bapaume Road, is the Tommy Café, its windows full of decorated artillery shell cases, and its garden transformed into a line of trenches and dugouts stuffed with every kind of military equipment, including shell-case gas gongs and German helmets used as flower-pots. It is yet another irony in a story full of ironies, that it is these (and other) café-museums which attract today's tourists in ever increasing numbers. Even though those with a direct personal experience of the Great War are almost gone, a new generation is visiting the old Western Front battlefields. Throughout the year, and during the summer especially, car parks are choked with cars and coaches, and the café-museums themselves overflow with visitors. Yet, as they relax with a coffee or a beer, how many spare a moment to reflect on the living history of Trench Art that is all around them?

Fig 7.11: The replica 'Pozieres Trench' at the Tommy Café at Pozieres on the Somme. Note the genuine gas-gong shell hanging from the dugout roof beam.

EPILOGUE

Great War Trench Art, in all its shapes and forms, serves as a bridge between three different and ultimately irreconcilable notions of the war: the 'lived' experience of soldiers, the second-hand views of those who read censored letters and propaganda newspaper accounts, and the bereaved, whose shattering sense of loss and grief at losing their loved ones so young can today be hardly imagined. In these few sentences are encapsulated the spectrum of our most intense human emotions.

In *Some Reflections of a Soldier*, R.H. Tawney comments how, on returning home from the front, he felt like a visitor among strangers, separated from his family by a veil unconsciously made by those who 'are afraid of what may happen to [their] souls if you expose them to the inconsistencies and contradictions, the doubts and bewilderment, which lie beneath the surface of things.' Trench Art, it seems, is an eloquent testimony to many of those inconsistencies and contradictions, a physical embodiment of the confusion of pain, pride and endurance, that befell so many families during and after the Great War.

Trench Art is best known from the First World War and hence this book has focused on objects from this conflict and its aftermath. Yet, by its very nature, Trench Art defies our ability to fully understand its diversity, or to decipher completely the messages that cleave to its materials, shapes and techniques of production. Modern war changes people and objects, and reveals how, through its concentrated intensities, it can redefine the social, spiritual and physical worlds which humans create and inhabit. Trench Art was to be a feature of almost every twentieth century conflict, and a book could be written on every one. What this little volume hopefully has shown, is that few kinds of material culture symbolized the human aspects of the Great War so well, or have endured so long, as the objects we call Trench Art.

THE MARKET FOR TRENCH ART
AND PRICE GUIDE

Today there is a ground-swell of interest in the many different kinds of Trench Art, both scholarly and commercially. The growing market includes a number museums who are re-assessing the historical significance of the material and adding to their collections, as well as specialist private collectors and those interested more generally in militaria. This is an international phenomenon which shows no signs of diminishing.

Though currently less popular than, say, edged weapons or firearms, for which there is a larger and longer established market, Trench Art is increasingly sought after, and even in the past few years has become comparatively more difficult to find. Yet, the market for Trench Art is as fragmented and difficult to pin down as the history of the genre itself. The range of objects is so wide that there will always be items which appeal to one or other kind of collector, and for a variety of reasons.

Trench Art is collected by those who are interested in it for its own sake, but also by enthusiasts fascinated by only one kind of object. Those interested in aeroplanes, ships, tanks, or smoking equipment,

Fig. I: One of the many regular militaria fairs held in the U.K.

Fig. 2: Random selection of Trench Art shell cases at a militaria fair.

Fig. 3: High price item. This masterpiece, made by the Versavel brothers, would command a premium if it came up for sale, due to its craftsmanship and history.
Author copyright with acknowledgemnet to the Versavel Archive.

Fig. 4: Though this Trench Art windmill has no provenience it's distinctiveness would attract a high price.

will often purchase a few items of Trench Art so as to add an unusual piece to their collections. Similarly, those who collect only woodwork, or beadwork, embroideries, or memorabilia of a specific regiment, may well acquire a Trench Art example to spice up their collections. Many of these collectors have little interest in Trench Art beyond their own focus of interest. Partly as a consequence, these particular items appear under different headings of collectables. Their usually higher prices reflect their value to the specialist collector rather than having been established by those interested in Trench Art as such. In other words, different spheres of collecting overlap in Trench Art, adding further volatility to the market.

Apart from the de-stabilising effect on prices which these cross-cutting collecting habits have had in recent years there are more traditional concerns. As with all collectables, prices for Trench Art vary considerably according to the visual attractiveness and completeness of the item and the place where one purchases it. The same decorated artillery shell case can be sold for £10 or less in a car boot sale, £20-£30 in a militaria fair, and upwards of £70 in an established antiques shop. Location also counts, as a small local 'junk' or antiques shop will sell items far cheaper than similar outlets in big cities. Consequently there is a lot of scope for acquiring good pieces at a fair

Fig. 5: Trench Art, edged weapons, belts, and assorted memorabilia at a militaria fair at Albert on the Somme, April 1999.

Fig. 6: Elaborately shaped and engraved 'writing set' made from cut brass on sale at a French militaria sale.

Fig. 7: A 'new' old kind of Trench Art. These souvenir key-rings are newly made from original Great War .303 bullets and pieces of copper drive-bands, and have recently re-appeared for sale in the Belgian city of Ieper (Ypres).

price if one is willing to hunt around.

Internationally, prices also vary considerably. In flea markets and local militaria fairs in France and Belgium, fine examples of almost every kind of Trench Art discussed in this book can be found for prices between half and a third of what one would pay for the same item in the United Kingdom, though again prices are rising. It is also possible to stumble across interesting examples in many places one visits on holiday. Great War Trench Art (and that from the Second World War) has been reported for sale in the Caribbean, Greece, Turkey, Israel, Egypt, and various Eastern European countries. Such items can also be found in Canada, Australia and New Zealand. As one might expect, the United States is a vast and specialized market in its own right, where interest in Great War Trench Art is part of a wider fascination which includes objects from the American Civil War, Spanish-American War, and the conflict in Vietnam.

The Internet reflects, and in a peculiar way highlights, the worldwide fluctuation of Trench Art prices. It is possible to see often virtually identical items being sold for, say, $10 and $30, or $60 and $250, on the same auction website. Almost always there is little verification available as to what the piece is, where it comes from, or to what category it belongs, though spectacular exceptions do occur. Buyers in general have to rely on overused and vague descriptions such as 'unique', 'distinctive', 'unusual' - words which give little clue as to whether the object was made by a soldier or civilian, during or after the war.

The main reason for the hitherto hit-and-miss nature of Trench Art collecting and its wildly fluctuating prices has been the lack of any scholarly research or books on the subject. With no way of classifying or categorizing the material, many buyers and sellers are often unable to make a reasoned judgement as to what it is they are purchasing and why it might be more or less historically significant or valuable. In the absence of such knowledge, and of an established commercial baseline, prices have tended to reflect the individual desires of the seasoned collector, supply and demand, and the values given to pieces which appear associated with other better known areas of collecting such as those mentioned above, or with those whose interest is in memorabilia from pre-Great War conflicts, such as the Napoleonic, American Civil or Boer wars. To date, and in general, 20th century Trench Art has only been worth what someone is willing to pay.

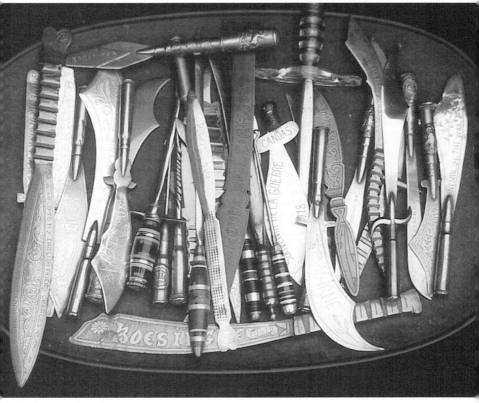

Fig. 8: A tray full of memories.

During the course of my research many people have commented that, by producing a long sought after categorization, and discussing the significance of different kinds of Great War Trench Art, this book would provide not only a history of these objects, but also a commercial baseline - a structure for assessing items and assigning a reasoned scale of prices. In the past, similar books on other hitherto unpublished kinds of militaria have led to an explosion of interest and a rise in prices as some method and discipline was introduced to the market. This may well prove to be the case with Trench Art, albeit reinforced by the increasing scarcity of objects as time goes by. It is hoped that, at the very least, any increase in commercial value will entail also an appreciation of the distinctive historical values of Trench Art as a unique kind of artistic endeavour.

This book is described as a history and guide - a guide to types of Trench Art, their makers and the stories they tell. Although not intended as a collectors' price guide, it has been decided to include a general outline of commercial values for the main kinds of Trench Art which have been encountered during the research for this book.

The prices given here are for good condition pieces from the United Kingdom only, and relate to the middle of the range, i.e. militaria fairs, rather than cheaper car-boot sales or overly expensive antiques shops. These prices should be not be regarded as definitive, and should be used warily and in light of my comments on the developing status of the Trench Art market. A reasonable guess is that prices will increase at around ten percent annually. New collectors should always bear in mind the condition and completeness of the item, check for signs of repair, and look for any dates or names carried by the piece, as these enhance its overall value. Hopefully also, some of those who buy Trench Art will do so on the basis of the social and cultural importance which every item possesses. In other words, to see them for what they truly are – unique pieces of history.

Shell cases:	£30-£40, depending on condition and degree of decoration. Expect to pay a premium for a pair.
Letter-openers:	£10-£15, depending on condition and degree of decoration.
Bullet pens/pencils:	£20-£25, depending on whether the piece has pen and/or pencil element.
Lighters:	£15-£30. Take care to note whether the flint-wheel revolves and whether the item has been repaired.
Matchbox holders:	£12-£15 for simple designs and £15-£20 for more elaborate examples, e.g. with bullet or copper element inlays.
Bullet-crucifixes:	£25-£35, depending on how elaborate the item is.
Aeroplanes:	£40-£60. Take care to look for breakages and repairs, especially on biplane and tri-plane examples.

Beadwork snakes:	£50-£80. These are rare.
Metal tanks:	£40-£50 for good quality and unusual examples and £15-£20 for more basic items.
Wooden tanks:	£30-£35 for plain wooden examples and £50-£60 for examples which incorporate metal elements.
Finger rings:	£5-£10 for most examples, £10-£20 for unusual examples, e.g. with inlays.

Websites:

Type 'Trench Art' into any search engine on the Internet and there will appear many websites which offer a miscellany of items for viewing and sale, though most have only a handful of pieces, and are usually accompanied by minimum details and rather basic photographs. The Trench Art surfer should also regularly check the several dedicated internet auction sites and especially the websites of established militaria auction houses such as Wallis and Wallis at www.wallisandwallis.co.uk.

Although these sites cater for most tastes and pockets, it is nevertheless clear that there is a large and growing international interest in Trench Art, on all levels, from historical to the artistic as well as the commercial. In an attempt to remedy the previous neglect of Trench Art in cyberspace as well as in more traditional forms, my own website aims to be a focus for all who have an interest in this subject. Located at **www.trenchart.net** my hope is that this will be the expert website on Trench Art and first port of call for anyone who is interested in any aspect of this material.

As with all websites it is undergoing constant development. Currently it carries a selection of images from my photographic archive, excerpts from my published work, and items of interest to those who are interested in visiting museums with Trench Art exhibits. The hope is that visitors will send information on their collections, unusual pieces, family Trench Art with a history, web links, and photographs on any kind of Trench Art, from any war, anywhere in the world. This can be sent electronically to the email address given on the website or by writing to the author c/o Pen and Sword Books.

SOURCE OF QUOTATIONS

Chapter 3

1/ 'While you are at the front ...'. Mrs Alec Tweedie, quoted in, *Fighting Forces, Writing Women: Identity and Ideology in the First World War*, S. Ouditt, 1994, London: Routledge, p 74.

Chapter 6

1/ 'Showers of lead flying about ...'. Dorothy Scoles, quoted in *Dismembering the Male*, J. Bourke, 1996, London: Reaktion Books, p 76.

2/ '... was a vision indescribable ...'. Sergeant H.E. May, quoted in, *True World War 1 Stories*, J.E. Lewis (ed.), 1997, London: Robinson Publishing, p 200.

3/ '... an expert knowledge of all ..'. Private A. Paterson, quoted in, *True World War 1 Stories*, J.E. Lewis (ed.), 1997, London: Robinson Publishing, p 239.

4/ 'Napper was found dead ...'. *The War the Infantry Knew 1914-1919*, Captain J.C. Dunn, [1938] 1997, London: Abacus, p 527.

5/ 'Ladies and Gentlemen this is High Wood...', Philip Johnston, quoted in, *Tourism, Pilgrimage, and the Commemoration of the Great War in Great Britain, Australia and Canada, 1919-1939*, D. Lloyd, 1994, PhD Thesis, Cambridge University, p 55.

6/ 'Yes, that thing by the fireplace...'. *Auntie Mabel's War*, M. Wenzel and J. Cornish, 1980, London: Allen Lane, p 8.

7/ 'French 75mm Shell Case sent home...'. *William Henry Goss: The Story of the Staffordshire Family of Potters who Invented Heraldic Porcelain*, L. and N. Pine, 1987, Milestone Publications, p 137.

8/ '... a Modernist method that...'. *A War Imagined*, S. Hynes, 1990, London: The Bodley Head, p 195.

9/ 'The war has figuratively...'. Camille Mauclair, quoted in, *Esprit de Corps*, K.E. Silver, London: Thames and Hudson, p 27.

Epilogue

1/ '... are afraid of what ...'. R. H. Tawney, quoted in, *A War Imagined*, S. Hynes, 1990, London: The Bodley Head, p 116.

BIBLIOGRAPHY

Anon. 1915. Les Bagues des Tranchées. *L'Illustration* No. 3771, 3 July 1915: 20

Appadurai, A. (ed.), 1986. *The Social Life of Things.* Cambridge: Cambridge University Press.

AWMM. 1922. *A Guidebook for the use of visitors.* Melbourne and Sydney: Australian War Memorial Museum.

Baert, K. et al. 1999. *In Flanders Fields Museum: Catalogue of the Objects.* Ieper: In Flanders Fields Museum.

Becker, A. 1996. *Croire.* Péronne: Historial de la Grande Guerre.

Bourke, J. 1996. *Dismembering the Male: Men's Bodies, Britain and the Great War.* London: Reaktion Books.

Caunt, P.M. 1998. *Military Sweetheart Jewellery II.* London: ARBRAS.

Comus, S. 1997. Trench Art. *Gun World,* August 1997:20-23

Cork, R. 1994. *A Bitter Truth: Avant-Garde Art and the Great War.* New Haven: Yale University Press.

Cresswell, Y.M. (ed.). 1994. *Living with the Wire: Civilian Internment in the Isle of Man during the two World Wars.* Douglas: Manx National Heritage, The Manx Museum & National Trust.

Degaast, M.G. 1917. La bijouterie des tranchées. *Almanach Illustré du Petit Parisien.*: 99-104.

Depoorter, Ch., Cossey, S. and Tillie, W. 1999. 1914-1918: De *Oorlog Achter Het Front; The War Behind the Front.* Poperinge: 'Aan de Schreve'/Ieper: Vansevenant nv.

Dunn, J.C. 1997 [1938]. *The War the Infantry Knew 1914-1919: A Chronicle of Service in France and Belgium.* London: Abacus.

Hynes, S. 1990. *A War Imagined: The First World War and English Culture.* London: The Bodley Head.

Illustrated War News. 1916. Useful articles made from Zeppelin wreckage'. *Illustrated War News* December 6th 1916, Part 26 (New Series):14

Jones, B. and B. Howells, B. 1972. *Popular Arts of the First World War.* London: Studio Vista.

Kwint, M. 1998. *Images and Reflections: Pleasure and Pastime, 1914-1918.* In, People's Century: Continuity Series.: 241-263. London and Bicester: BBC/BCS.

Lewis, J.E. (ed.). 1997. *True World War 1 Stories: Sixty Personal Narratives of the War*. London: Robinson Publishing.

Lloyd, D.W. 1998. *Battlefield Tourism: Pilgrimage and the Commemoration of the Great War in Britain, Australia and Canada, 1919-1939*. Oxford: Berg Publishers.

Lyndhurst, J. 1983. *Military Collectibles: An international directory of twentieth-century militaria*. Leicester: Magna Books/Salamander Books.

Maas, B. and Dietrich, G. 1994. *Lebenszeichen: Schmuck aus Notzeiten*. Köln: Museum für Angewandte Kunst.

Meistrell, D.E. 1976. 'Trench Vases': Fancy, Engraved, Etched, or Hand Hammered Brass Artillery Shell Casings. *No attribution*: 26-7

Methley, J.L.H. 1939. His Wallet is Stuffed with Souvenirs: A Wartime 'Tommy' Goes Over Some Relics. *Yorkshire Evening Post*, Friday 12 May 1939.

R.W. 1915. Trench Trinkets: Souvenirs soldiers make from German shells. First Anniversary of the War Special Number; 5 August 1915. *The War Budget* IV (12):361.

Rickards, M. and M. Moody. 1975. *The First World War: Ephemera, Mementoes and Documents*. Jupiter.

Rohe, P.J. 1979. Trench Art Treasure. *Hobbies-The Magazine for Collectors* July 1979: 91-2

Saunders, N.J. 2000a. Bodies of metal, shells of memory: 'Trench Art' and the Great War Re-cycled. *Journal of Material Culture*, 5 (1):43-67.

Saunders, N.J. 2000b. Trench Art: The Recyclia of War. In J. Coote, C. Morton, and J. Nicholson (eds), Transformations: *The Art of Recycling*.: 64-67. Oxford: Pitt-Rivers Museum.

Saunders, N.J. 2000c. Memories of Metal: Trench Art, a lost resource of the Great War. *Stand To!* The Journal of the Western Front Association. 58: 14-17.

Saunders, N.J. 2000d. Trench Art: collecting history, retailing memories. *The Armourer* 42:40-43.

Saunders, N.J. 2001a. Matter and memory in the landscapes of conflict: The Western Front 1914-1999. In, B. Bender and M. Winer (eds), *Contested Landscapes, and Landscapes of Migration and Exile*. Oxford: Berg Publishers.

Saunders, N.J. 2001b. Apprehending Memory: Material Culture and War, 1919-1939. In, P.H. Liddle and H. Cecil (eds), *Lightning*

Strikes Twice: Personal Experiences of two World Wars: London. HarperCollins.

Saunders, N.J. In Press. The Ironic Culture of Shells in the Great War. In, J. Schofield, W.G. Johnson, and C. Beck (eds), *Matériel Culture: The Archaeology of 20th Century Conflict.*: London: Routledge.

Saunders, N.J. In preparation. *Trench Art: Materialities and Memories of War.* Oxford: Berg Publishers.

Saunders, N.J. and P. Cornish. In preparation. Hoarding Art, collecting memories: 'Trench Art' from the Imperial War Museum.

Silver, K.E. 1989. *Esprit de Corps: Art of the Parisian Avante-garde and the First World War, 1914-25.* London: Thames and Hudson.

Stewart, S. 1993. *On Longing: Narratives of the Miniature, the Gigantic, the Souvenir, the Collection.* Durham: Duke University Press.

Vermeulen-Roose, G. (Comp.). 1972. *Van Obushuls tot Sierstuk: Studie over een originale en Kunstvolle Vrijetijdsbesteding onder de oorlog 1914-1918.* Zonnebeke: De Zonnebekse Heemvrienden.

Wenzel, M. and Cornish, J. (comps.). 1980. *Auntie Mabel's War: An account of her part in the hostilities of 1914-18.* London: Allen Lane.

Whalen, R.W. 1984. *Bitter Wounds: German Victims of the Great War, 1914-1939.* Ithaca: Cornell University Press.

Winter, J. 1995. Sites of Memory, Sites of Mourning: The Great War in European cultural history. Cambridge: Cambridge University Press.

'Killing Time'

University of Plymouth Library

Subject to status this item may be renewed
via your Voyager account

http://voyager.plymouth.ac.uk

Exeter tel: (01392) 475049
Exmouth tel: (01395) 255331
Plymouth tel: (01752) 232323